ROOSEVELT READS

GLIMMERS OF UNDERSTANDING FROM
AN ENTHUSIASTIC READER

MARK ROOSEVELT

This collection of essays is brought to you by Antioch College. If it inspires you to help the College with our future endeavors, please visit **donate.antiochcollege.org.**

Roosevelt Reads
Glimmers Of Understanding From An Enthusiastic Reader
Copyright © 2015 Mark Roosevelt
All rights reserved.

Publishing by Ertel Publishing, Inc.
www.ertelpublishing.com

ISBN: 978-0-692-20765-9

CONTENTS

Introduction—Maxwell King **5**

A Note of Explanation **8**

AUTHORS

My Favorite Books—John Updike's Rabbit Novels **10**

Jolts of Apprehension—Richard Ford's Bascombe Trilogy **16**

Graham Greene's "Fundamental Trembling" **22**

Living Alone and the Novels of Anita Brookner **24**

A Trip to Montana and Richard Hugo **29**

Regret, "Looking Back," and Doris Grumbach **33**

Struggling in the System and Wendell Berry's Lonely Agrarian Vision **38**

Loss, Grief, and Sonali Deraniyagala's *Wave* **46**

The Discovery of Patrick O'Brian **49**

"Down These Mean Streets a Man Must Go"—Raymond Chandler **55**

Giving Up on the Dream of Success—Jim Harrison and Jim Gavin **59**

"A Brief for the Defense"—the Poetry of Jack Gilbert **64**

HISTORY

"Look into his Beautiful Eyes"—Abraham Lincoln **71**

Books about Lincoln **80**

The Obstinate Leadership of Charles De Gaulle **84**

An "ice-axe to the soul," the Bloodlands of Eastern Europe **89**

It Did Not Need to Be That Way—the Service of Wendell Willkie **95**

The Best President of Our Lifetime? **102**

The Roosevelts **106**

CURRENT EVENTS

The Rise of Women, Inequality, and Our Timid Politics **115**

Some Good News and Worries about Higher Education **121**

The Cost of Growth—*The Sixth Extinction* and *The End of the Wild* **126**

A Defining Moment, Hardly Noticed **134**

MISCELLANEOUS

Reckoning with America—Surprising New Television **137**

Music and the Pleasures of "Lesser Lights" **143**

Baseball **148**

Holiday Thoughts—"What We Need is Here" **154**

INTRODUCTION

THE CONCEPT of the literary review—first applied to books and then to cinema, television, music, and virtually every aspect of our modern culture—is as varied as culture itself. It has ranged from the pedestrian—the book or movie reviewer who offers little insight but monotonously recites the entire plot, thus ruining rather than enhancing the experience—to the sublime social criticism of intellectuals like Malcolm Cowley, whose literary criticism in the 1930s helped shape the era of Fitzgerald, Hemingway, and Wolfe, and whose social criticism was so trenchant and left-leaning as to pique the interest of J. Edgar Hoover and the FBI.

Mark Roosevelt's "Roosevelt Reads" columns fall into the sublime category and are reminiscent of great minds like Cowley—not so much in the leaning left as the exceptional range and heft of Roosevelt's views. His voracious reading habit—the man usually has several books going, inhabits a house overflowing with volumes, and often sends dinner guests away with reading assignments—informs a sensibility that ranges over current culture, the important issues and challenges of our time, and history and biography.

It is Roosevelt's breadth of experience and active participation in the world that provides the fodder for his fertile brain. He has battled. As a legislator in Massachusetts he passed landmark gay rights legislation and authored the nation's most comprehensive—and effective—educational reform law. After a bruising defeat in his campaign for governor, instead of retreating, he embraced even more challenging work. He served over five years as superintendent of schools in Pittsburgh, Pennsylvania, where he advanced bold reforms that are still bearing fruit for that community and inspired and developed The Pittsburgh Promise Scholarship Fund, perhaps the most ambitious college scholarship program in the country.

Today he serves as the president of Antioch College in Yellow Springs, Ohio. At Antioch, Roosevelt has led the effort to rebirth one of America's most distinguished academic institutions and has crafted a breathtakingly ambitious vision for a college dedicated to innovative twenty-first-century learning and green design. The creativity Roosevelt has put into his vision for Antioch is reflected in the range of the "Roosevelt Reads" columns he has been writing for the College's publications and website for the past three years.

Roosevelt often digresses from books to other forms, as most thoughtful critics do. He comments on demographic trends, offers a "Roosevelt Listens" column on the virtues of less well-known composers such as Boccherini and Tartini, and detours into film and even television. One of the strongest columns deals with the PBS series on the Roosevelt family (Yes, Mark is the great-grandson of Teddy). He uses his own experience, his grasp of the Roosevelt character, and his sharply drawn understanding of American history and society to weave a powerful experience for the reader that both complements and enhances the experience of watching the Ken Burns series. And all this in a writerly style that might even have pleased the very picky Cowley.

INTRODUCTION

But it is on the subject of books—books, books, books—that Roosevelt is most inspiring. Politics and education have been the stuff of his life's work, but books are a great passion of his life. And his ability to find meaning, nuance, and insight in them makes for great reading.

These columns were written for a small audience and, like the best literary correspondence of years past, possess the feeling of sharing enthusiasms and observations with friends. Because there are more than a few of us involved with Antioch who eagerly await these monthly "Roosevelt Reads" installments, the College decided to compile them in book form, to share with those involved with the resurrection of Antioch and also a wider audience.

Mark Roosevelt is a fine writer and keen observer. It is a true pleasure to see these reviews gathered in book form for readers who admire his thinking.

—MAXWELL KING

Maxwell King is president and CEO of The Pittsburgh Foundation and a member of the Antioch College Board of Trustees. Mr. King's career has included time as an editor and writer on newspapers and magazines, leadership of two important institutions in the American philanthropic community, and service on numerous civic boards and committees. He served almost eight years as the editor of *The Philadelphia Inquirer* in the 1990s, nine years as the president of The Heinz Endowments, and six years on the board of the National Council on Foundations, including two years as chair. Mr. King received his Bachelor of Arts degree cum laude from Harvard University in 1967, and attended the Stanford Executive Program at Stanford University's Graduate School of Business. He is also a published poet.

A NOTE OF EXPLANATION

I AM OBSESSED with books. Our house is full of them, as is my office. I do not use a Kindle or Nook—I enjoy the feel and texture of a book and love how they look on the shelves. Books make any room more attractive and weighty. And I like to own books rather than borrow them.

I also care about the condition of a book. Persnickety? That might be too mild. I like a book to remain clean, with an unbroken binding, so I read with the book open no more than 90 degrees and use a bookmark rather than turning down the page corners. This feels normal to me, although I realize it might not to you.

I am influenced by book design and appearance. It affects my purchasing choices, and it also affects the pleasures I get from a particular book. It is as if the book I am reading is for a time my living room, and the book cover is a prominent picture on the wall of that room.

I read at night after I go to bed. If I am anxious about something, reading helps me focus on someone else's problems, which allows me to sleep better. Reading also helps me feel less alone. Authors I have been reading for a very long time become friends of a sort, often rather intimate friends. Reading is about searching, often for knowledge or entertainment, but also for things we have lost or wish we had. Many of my favorite authors are older men approaching the age of my father. He would be 99 were he still alive, and we were not as close as I would have liked.

A NOTE OF EXPLANATION

I read fiction, history, biography, and a good bit of poetry. I also read books that address issues I am dealing with in my work life. I try to read books written by authors with different worldviews than mine.

I feel better when I am reading regularly and, if I am not reading, tend to feel an absence, as if someone I am very close to is away on an extended vacation.

I am not a cultural critic or a professor of literature, just an enthusiastic reader. Writing this column has provided the opportunity to add further meaning to a lifetime of reading and constant clipping and filing of quotes, articles, or thoughts that intrigue me.

After all this reading I am amazed by how little I know, and as I age, by how little I remember. And I have come to believe that is where the pursuit of knowledge should lead us—to a place of humility. An understanding that what matters most is beyond our grasp. That books and music and other art forms at their best offer glimmers of understanding and illumination. And that is all we can hope for.

—MARK ROOSEVELT

AUTHORS

MY FAVORITE BOOKS—
JOHN UPDIKE'S RABBIT NOVELS

A GREAT MANY things happen as you age. Time grows shorter and options diminish or are eliminated. Health challenges mount. But there are many positives as well. You learn to spend your time more carefully, not to waste emotional energy, to savor and harbor, and to distill what really matters.

There are many books that matter a great deal to me, or have at one time or another. And although I read history and biography, fiction is what I would have if I had just one shelf to fill.

Most good books hit home when you are ready for them to. For me, that has been especially true of many of the books I consider "great," such as *Middlemarch*, *War and Peace*, Mahfouz's *The Cairo Trilogy*, *Buddenbrooks*, *The Invisible Man*, *Moby Dick*, and Naipaul's *A House for Mr. Biswas*. I was not open to them, and then I was, and, at that time, they gave great joy. I cannot explain why this happens. I have still not been able to open myself to either Henry James or Faulkner, although I have tried multiple times. Perhaps those pleasures are still to come. And although I was once open to Hemingway, for example, I no longer am, even though I happily gobble up books by some of his literary successors, such as Thomas McGuane and Jim Harrison. And it is not always me that changes; some writers change greatly and become more appealing. I did not enjoy early Philip Roth, but love his later books, especially many of the recent short novels that distill a lifetime into two hundred pages.

Some authors have meant a great deal to me for a very long time, among them Willa Cather (*The Professor's House* might be my single favorite novel), Nadine Gordimer, William Maxwell, Patrick O'Brian, William Trevor, and Richard Yates.

WILLA CATHER, AROUND 1912
Willa Cather Pioneer Memorial and Educational Foundation

But if I had to choose the books that matter most to me, they would be Updike's Rabbit novels (*Rabbit, Run*; *Rabbit Redux*; *Rabbit is Rich*; *Rabbit at Rest*; and the novella *Rabbit Remembered*), and Richard Ford's Frank Bascombe trilogy (*The Sportswriter*, *Independence Day*, and *The Lay of the Land*), which I will write about in next month's column. These books help explain America to me, an America that I have inhabited, as well as the times in which I have lived. I realize that this is in large part due to who and what I am—a white man born in the 1950s—and that these books might not be as evocative for other people. They locate me in a time and a place, more luminous and yet also darker than I had realized.

Much has been written about what to make of John Updike. He has been extravagantly praised as the greatest American writer of the twentieth century with a prose style of unsurpassed clarity and beauty. And he has been vilified as sex-obsessed; the late novelist David Foster Wallace called him a "champion literary phallocrat" serving as "both chronicler and voice of probably the most self-absorbed generation since Louis XIV." And conservative cultural critic Norman Podhoretz describes him as a writer "whose authentic emotional range is so narrow and thin that it may without too much exaggeration be characterized as limited to a rather timid nostalgia for the confusions of youth."

Although it strikes me as odd that he is the object of so much hostility, especially as he was generally modest, even self-deprecating about his own limitations, it is possible that all of the above observations are true. Updike's prose is at times shatteringly beautiful, but he often writes rather embarrassingly about sex. He created many one-dimensional female characters and is of that generation whose conservative beginnings were shattered by a newfound and often over-utilized sexual freedom, without significant contemplation of the many unwanted consequences. All of the above is part of him and his work.

He also wrote too much, publishing sixty books in his lifetime, causing someone to remark that he never had an "unpublished thought." As might be expected from such a prolific writer, he authored many mediocre—even bad—books, several of which I have been unable to finish. He wrote books about art and golf, a science fiction novel (*Towards the End of Time*), an experimental novel (*Seek My Face*), a magical realism novel (*Brazil*), three novels riffing off *The Scarlet Letter* (*A Month of Sundays*, *Roger's Version*, and *S.*), three novels based on a fictional Jewish writer (*Bech a Book*, *Bech is Back*, and *Bech at Bay*), and a novel about an African dictatorship (*The Coup*). He published six massive volumes of assorted nonfiction, as well as eight books of poetry.

But after culling what is insubstantial, you are left with a body of work perhaps unsurpassed in the late twentieth century. He wrote one of the greatest baseball essays, "Hub Fans Bid Kid Adieu" about Ted Williams' final game. He wrote several small volumes of lyrical short stories of tremendous insight and compassion. Note particularly the stories about the Maples, documenting the gentle early rhythms and painful dissolution of a first marriage, and the end-of-life gems of reflection and regret in his final volume, *My Father's Tears and Other Stories*. He wrote poetry that at its best, such as in his last volume, *Endpoint and Other Poems*, had what critic Charles McGrath called "another, deeper music." And he wrote a great late novel, *In the Beauty of the Lilies*, a sad, wrenching generational saga that would be the stand-out work of almost any other writer's career.

And he wrote the Rabbit books.

To contemplate Updike is to contemplate an America that existed in its distinctive form for only part of the fifties, sixties, and seventies, and for only a select group of people—mostly male, heterosexual, and white. "My subject is the American Protestant small town middle class," Updike wrote. "I like middles. It is in middles that extremes clash, where ambiguity restlessly rules."

He also once wrote that "America is a vast conspiracy to make you happy." And perhaps for a time Updike really did believe that. But his fiction is nuanced and often dark, and happiness and stability prove as elusive in his small Pennsylvania or New England towns as it does anywhere else. And while most of his male characters are perhaps of "a type," and mostly just alternative views of himself, he takes them deep.

Updike was not a political writer, nor was he a very political person. But he had a profound if limited sense for whom he spoke. Very early in his career he determined that he would speak in a distinctly American voice for an American audience. He rejected the need to mimic a modernist European ethos. He believed America needed authors "who are filled with the strength of their cultures and do not transcend the limits of their age, but working within the times, bring what is peculiar to the moment to glory…who love their environments with such vitality that they can produce an epic out of the Protestant ethic."

And that he did. The Rabbit books will stand as a heart-stoppingly accurate portrayal of how life was lived by many Americans of the age through the story of Harry "Rabbit" Angstrom. High school basketball star and car salesman, Rabbit is coping, barely, with the social and cultural changes unfolding around him. The

British novelist Ian McEwan says that in the Rabbit books Updike "touched at points on the Shakespearean." The aspirations, illusions, justifications, disappointments, and anxieties, as well as the hard-won successes and the probably more lasting and dispiriting failures, are all there. Because of that, the books can be painful to read, especially when Rabbit's delusions and limitations mirror one's own. But Updike's affection for Rabbit and for the scrappy Pennsylvania towns he inhabits comes through not because he protects them from scrutiny, but because he does not. He sees Rabbit whole and still loves him, later calling him "a brother to me, and a good friend."

Updike concluded that "whatever the failings of my work, let it stand as a manifesto of my love for the time in which I was born." He felt his "only duty was to describe reality as it has come to me, to give the mundane its beautiful due."

What a spectacular phrase that is—"to give the mundane its beautiful due." Not surprising that Updike describes his own work better than any critic. And how wonderful is his respectful attention to what so many others dismiss as banal and pedestrian.

I grew up reading Updike and have read him all my life. For me he was like the weather and baseball, part of the taken-for-granted landscape of my day-to-day existence. I miss him enormously and return to his best work often.

April 2012

JOLTS OF APPREHENSION—
RICHARD FORD'S BASCOMBE TRILOGY

THERE ARE MANY reasons to read, of which the most significant is illumination. Figuring out what life is about occupies our thoughts sooner or later, and those of us who are not religious look to writers to throw a little light on it all. Wallace Stevens wrote that "in an age of disbelief, it is for the poet to provide the satisfactions of belief with his measure and his style." Robert Frost described reading as "a momentary stay against confusion."

So, yes, while I often read to relax and to get my thoughts away from my worries, I mostly read to see things clearer and to feel less alone. Writers and their books have become long-term, rather intimate friends, sharing thoughts, fears, and dreams to an extent that is unusual except in the most intimate real-life relationships. Often when reading a good book, I will get a jolt or insight that makes something important a bit easier to understand. Sometimes that jolt comes from confronting something in my own life that I would have kept hidden away and that might otherwise only be revealed by one of those dreams in which your self-conscious leaves you no other choice.

When you have read a writer's work for a long time you feel that they are not only an old friend but that they are also your advance scout, experiencing and reporting back on what lies ahead. Walter Jackson Bate spent much of his life studying Samuel Johnson and said that reading his work was deeply consoling because "wherever you are going in life you will meet Johnson on his way back." John Updike has played that role for me, and the stories and poems written towards the end of his life move me greatly and help prepare me for what comes next. Many such late-life ruminations, full of longing, gratefulness, regret, and the struggle to hold on to what one has loved remind me that fear of death has more to do with losing one's memories, one's past, than with losing whatever future days might offer.

I have been reading Donald Hall's poetry since college. Following his path through his deeply personal poems and essays is similar to getting an honest, beautifully written annual holiday letter. I know of his struggles with career and an early divorce; his love of rural New Hampshire and his "smartest thing I ever did" relocation to live in the farmhouse his great-grandparents bought in 1865; his great joy in a healthy second marriage to the poet Jane Kenyon and his increasingly rewarding work; his own successful struggle with colon cancer; and Kenyon's early death from leukemia and Hall's painful struggle to find some joy in his last years living with her absence.

In terms of "jolts of apprehension," no writer has provided more than Richard Ford. His first two books were too hard-boiled for me. Some of his later work, including his most recent novel, *Canada*, is wonderful, and he has also written some spectacular short stories. But none of these works share the grand aspiration and achievement of the Frank Bascombe trilogy.*

---

* Since this was written, Ford has published a fourth volume, the very poorly titled *Let Me Be Frank With You*.

We are first introduced to Bascombe in *The Sportswriter*. A former fiction writer, Bascombe is numb and off-kilter as he grapples with the personal crisis resulting from the death of his young son, Ralph, from disease four years earlier and the subsequent end of his marriage. Ford likes setting his stories on holidays ("holidays are often when people want to be most themselves, when they want to be the best they can be") and *The Sportswriter* takes place during Easter week. As he attempts to regain his footing, Bascombe abandons fiction for sports writing, part of his attempt to embrace the ordinary. (Ford did just the opposite, leaving sports reporting to become a fiction writer.) But events or relations with other people keep making this transition difficult.

We meet Bascombe again in *Independence Day*, my favorite modern American novel, which takes place on July 4th weekend. He is now a real estate agent and in what Ford calls "the Existence Period," which is that time after the crises have subsided. He is on more solid ground, and the novel explores the cost of it, and whether and how he can again connect—really connect—to the people around him, in particular his fourteen-year-old son, Paul, and his girlfriend, Sally Caldwell.

There are so many parts of the book I relish—descriptions of characters and places, philosophical ramblings about America, fatherhood, real estate, almost anything. I will offer one passage and insight from the very beginning of the book that has stayed with me. It is an insight that has affected the way I look at the world, and it is in Ford's typical meandering style that frustrates a few, but pleases me immensely.

"A sad fact, of course, about adult life is that you see the very things that you'll never adapt to coming toward you on the horizon. You see them as the problems they are, you worry like hell about them, you make provisions, fashion adjustments; you tell yourself you'll have to change your way of doing things. Only you don't. You can't. Somehow it's already too late. And maybe it's even worse than that: maybe the thing you see coming from far away is not the real thing, the thing that scares you, but its aftermath. And what you've feared will happen has already taken place."

In other words, we spend most of our life in the "aftermath" dealing with things that have already happened, that cannot be undone, but we take so long to realize it that we do not get on with what can be done to adapt to the next approaching wave. Ford further notes, "And in that very way our life gets over before we know it. We miss it. And like the poet said: 'The ways we miss our lives are life.'"

The next volume in the trilogy is *The Lay of the Land*, which takes place at Thanksgiving in 2000, during the struggle to decide who won the Bush vs. Gore presidential election, which Ford has described elsewhere as "a time of peculiar moral lethargy." Bascombe is 55 and Sally Caldwell, now his wife, has left him to reunite with her first husband, who disappeared for decades after returning from Vietnam. Bascombe has been diagnosed with prostate cancer and is in what Ford calls his "Permanent Period." He has achieved a reasonable level of "acceptance" of his son's death and of his own life, although he still faces rough times. The novel explores what "acceptance" means and also what it means to be "thankful," just as the earlier novel explored what it means to be "independent." But this description makes the whole enterprise sound more contrived and analytical and less captivating than it really is.

Ford gives great interviews. He talks about what he is seeking to accomplish in his stories, about his own life, and how it connects to his books. His father died when he was sixteen, and he remarks that "it is always easy to write about things that go kaflooey, and people leave and the door slams and that's the dramatic end. But I am always interested in what happens after somebody walks out the door.... The most constructive impulse in my own life is that I don't ever walk out the door; I don't do exits...[b]ecause people left me when I was little. I never thought it was better to be alone than to be with someone you loved." Such interviews often cause me to dip into the novels again, usually just particular sections or episodes, and when I do, I am struck again by the beauty of the language and the emotional pull of Bascombe's struggles.

There is no escaping comparison to Updike's Rabbit books. In many ways Ford's trilogy picks up where Updike left off. Both Bascombe and Rabbit participate in and examine American middle class life (there is far more examining in Ford than in Updike) and absorb cultural shifts. Ford also embraces conventional narrative, and, like Updike, he writes exquisite sentences and is deeply respectful of his subject matter—America and its suburbs, yearnings, and sweet joys, as well as its many failings. Of course there are differences in tone and writing style, and Ford tells his story in the first person, whereas Updike writes in the third.

Ford and Updike were acquaintances, and Ford told Updike "that if he hadn't written those novels, I wouldn't have written mine. The fact that the Rabbit novels had such a large presence in American culture allowed me to think that such a thing could be done."

The most important similarity is in the scrupulous, loving attention to details of everyday life. Ford, like Updike, seeks "to give the mundane its beautiful due." At the beginning of *The Sportswriter*, Bascombe describes what life was like before his son died: "We paid bills, shopped, went to movies, bought cars and cameras and insurance, cooked out…stood in my yard and watched sunsets with a sense of solace and achievement, cleaned my rain gutters, eyed my shingles, put up storms, fertilized regularly…spoke to my neighbors in an interested voice—the normal applauseless life of us all."

"The normal applauseless life of us all" that Bascombe ran from when it no longer made sense and then had such trouble getting back to. The life we all struggle to come to terms with, and that literature, at its best as in the Bascombe books, can help us understand just a little bit better.

May 2012

GRAHAM GREENE'S "FUNDAMENTAL TREMBLING"

I JUST FINISHED Pico Iyer's *The Man Within My Head*. The man in question is the great British novelist Graham Greene. Iyer never met Greene, but found himself at quite an early age greatly affected by his writings and influenced by his worldview. He thinks about him a great deal and, especially when traveling, contemplates what Greene would make of various things. Iyer views Greene as an adopted father and much of the book is about how different his relationship is to his actual father. It is "only through another," Iyer comments, that you can "see yourself with shocking clarity. A real father is too close for comfort."

Greene was wary of power and of innocence, and the combination scared him most of all. He especially feared American power because he believed it to be dangerously innocent, as it is not steeped in an understanding of history and human limitations. He feared the consequences of zealotry and righteousness, and was more fearful of people whose motivations are seemingly altruistic than those with more obviously self-serving ambitions. He dealt in the dark shadows of how mistakes are made and pain is administered. An enemy cannot really hurt you. Only a friend can betray you.

Although I enjoyed it immensely, I hesitate to recommend Iyer's book because it is so much in my sweet spot that I am unsure what another reader will make of it. But I can recommend reading

Graham Greene's books, in particular *The Quiet American*, Iyer's favorite, and *The Heart of the Matter*.

They are both beautiful, sad books, full of Greene's trademark world-weariness. The main characters are mostly foreigners in their new homes, Vietnam and Sierra Leone, struggling to make sense of each other and where they fit in their adopted country.

The Quiet American was not originally well-received in our country, as it is highly critical of American influence and character. Robert Stone, an American novelist who shares many of Greene's preoccupations, writes in an introduction to the book that "innocence is a problem for all Americans in the novel and more of a problem for those who have to deal with them." Stone notes that Greene's anger about this is ferocious. The jaded Englishman, Fowler, says of the lead American character, Pyle, "He'll always be innocent, you can't blame the innocent, they are always guiltless. All you can do is control or eliminate them. Innocence is a kind of insanity."

"I never met a man who had better motives for all the trouble he caused," Fowler later said of Pyle.

Both books are about politics and religion, but as Iyer notes, there is something even more profound going on under the surface. He believes Greene was aware that such matters "were mere symptoms of some fundamental trembling."

That "fundamental trembling" is what makes Greene's best books so affecting.

February 2012

LIVING ALONE AND THE NOVELS
OF ANITA BROOKNER

I OFTEN WONDER why so little attention is given to the remarkable demographic changes happening in America and much of the rest of the "developed" world. One such change is the 33 percent increase in the number of adults living alone from 1996 to 2006, the last year for which we have reliable statistics.

My interest in this matter is sparked by several new books and a novelist who writes about characters who spend their adult lives alone and are decidedly unhappy about it.

The March 2, 2012, edition of the *New York Times Book Review* contains an informative review of *Going Solo: The Extraordinary Rise and Surprising Appeal of Living Alone* by Eric Klinenberg. As his title indicates, Klinenberg takes a generally positive view of the trend towards more single households, now 28 percent of the population. He says the data show that a majority of this group is female, that most are living alone because they want to, and that these singles are generally more socially engaged than married couples.

In his February 20, 2012 column, David Brooks of the *New York Times* riffed off Klinenberg's book to make an optimistic point about what he calls "the talent society." He notes that "fifty years ago America was groupy. People were more likely to be enmeshed in stable, dense and obligatory relationships…. Today individuals have more freedom," mostly because their relationships are more "loosely structured." He says that these looser arrangements mean that "we have gone from a society that protected people from their frailties to a society that allows people to maximize their talents." He argues that people were often stifled in the older social structures, and that now "they want more flexibility to explore their own interests and develop their own identities, lifestyles and capacities."

Count me as a bit of a skeptic, perhaps because I am very aware of my own human frailty and need for companionship.

I am also astonished that the plight of children is almost entirely absent from this discussion. Children are caught in the wake of these gigantic, and for them, primarily negative, social and demographic trends. I do not understand why commentators such as Brooks fail to connect the "freedom" stemming from these "loosely structured, more flexible relationships" to other demographic trends, such as divorce rates and the increase in single parenting. The *Times* reported on February 17, 2012, that for women under 30, a majority of births now occur outside of marriage. Ample research (note social historian Barbara Defoe Whitehead's 1997 book *The Divorce Culture* and her searing, painful vision of every divorce as the "death of a small civilization") indicates that children often flounder amidst the loosely structured relationships that contribute to this newfound adult freedom.

And is it really so clear that most women, especially later in life, are "choosing" to live alone? I wonder how much of this choice is connected to the negative behaviors found in men who are increasingly unable to comprehend, no less cope, with significant declines in their economic and educational status (again note Whitehead's work, in particular *Why There Are No Good Men Left*, 2002, and Kate Bolick's cover story in the November 2011 issue of the *Atlantic Magazine*, "All the Single Ladies").

Literature often reveals truths that social science misses, or at least different truths, and you won't find any reason for optimism about living alone in the writings of the British novelist Anita Brookner. Brookner, who won the 1984 Booker Prize for *Hotel Du Lac*, is prolific, having published nearly a novel a year from 1981 to 2006. She writes rather depressing novels about the inner lives of lonely people, usually in their fifties or beyond, mostly women, but men too, for whom the main psychological action is in accepting that their life is drawing to a close and that they have made "a hash of it." Most of her protagonists have not formed significant relationships or marriages, are without the consolation of children, and have spent a good part of their adult lives taking care of aging parents.

I have read many of her novels and just finished *Fraud*, one of her best. It is worth giving any number of her books a go, perhaps *Hotel Du Lac*, or *Latecomers*, her own favorite. In them, she is telling and retelling the same autobiographical story, and although I enjoy her books, reading too many in a short time can be tiresome.

Brookner is now in her mid-eighties, and a recluse. The few interviews she has given are extraordinarily forthright. As Mick Brown wrote in the *Telegraph* in 2009, "A conversation with her is like walking across Siberia—it may appear bleak and forbidding, but at the same time it is also shockingly, exhilaratingly bracing." Bracing in the way conversations are when no punches are pulled. Asked if she feels lonely by an interviewer for the *Paris Review*, Brookner replied, "Often. I have said that I am one of the loneliest women in London. People have resented it—it is not done to confess to loneliness, but there it is."

To Brookner, much literature is grossly misleading. The opening sentence of her first novel, *A Start in Life*, reads "Dr. Weiss, at 40, knew that her life had been ruined by literature." In Brookner's world, literature should reflect reality, which means that virtue is usually punished, the examined life is more painful, the hare beats the tortoise every time, and there are few if any happy endings. "Why?" she was asked by Mick Brown.

Because even "the body betrays you. And there is no escape. Age is the final betrayal."

Asked if "there is any coming to terms with that?" she responds, "Oh there is no consolation," as she fixes the interviewer with a piercing look. "You don't believe me do you? But it's true." She takes full responsibility for her own disappointments, believing not that life has been unfair to her, but that she has "made a hash of it." She wants to understand why and explores that in her novels. The consolation she offers, even if she cannot access it herself, is the consolation of looking at things straight on, with no blinders, or as she has said, "a peeling away of affectation."

Brookner's take on living alone is a sobering companion piece to the optimism of David Brooks' "Talent Society" and Klinenberg's *Going Solo*. Which you find more convincing likely depends on your own life experience. Klinenberg says that readers have vastly different responses to his book. He concludes that, "the topic of living alone is something like a Rorschach test: our reaction to it says as much about us as it does about the condition."

Of course many people can be happy living alone and many people are unhappy in marriage or other committed relationships. But aging alone can be extremely challenging (see Louis Begley's March 17 *Times* op-ed, "Age and Its Awful Discontents," and Diane Ackerman's insightful March 24 *Times* op-ed, "The Brain on Love") and as the nuclear family continues to erode as the primary structure for raising children, it is unclear to me what social constructs are replacing it and what that means for children's well-being.

Perhaps this transition to more people living alone will turn out well, but Brookner's stories give voice to many quietly unhappy people who often go unnoticed—an important role of novelists. As the British scholar Alfred Church wrote: "We are obliged to leave behind a trace of who we are and where we've come from and what we know—which of course changes constantly.... What can do that more truly than fiction writing? Nothing, in my opinion."

March 2012

A TRIP TO MONTANA AND RICHARD HUGO

I LOVE TO travel and love to read while on trips. Before a trip, I spend a few happy moments placing books "in nomination" and then choosing the ones that actually make it into my bags. Of course, a book that is connected in some way to my destination has an edge.

This summer Greg and Anne Avis invited my wife, Dorothy, daughter, Juliana, and me to visit their ranch about an hour and a half from Yellowstone (Greg is a member of the Antioch College Board of Trustees). Of course there are many fine books that are situated in Montana or similar western settings. I enjoy the nature-embracing, tough but injured, middle-aged guy books of Jim Harrison and Thomas McGuane and have read *A River Runs Through It* and much of Wallace Stegner with great pleasure. But I could find nothing "western" on my shelves that jumped out and said, "Read me now!" So I brought two books I had been meaning to read for years, Willa Cather's *Sapphira and the Slave Girl* and Jonathan Franzen's *The Corrections*.

The Avis' ranch proved to be as beautiful as we had heard. They have done a wonderful job converting existing buildings such as old granaries into two small, comfortable, and functional complexes that fit seamlessly into the landscape. Their architect says that they are doing what the land and its history call for, as a Montanan "would use what he had before he built something new," although of course the architect must know that is hardly true of most newcomers. They live at the edge of their large holding so that the rest of the property is as it was and, happily, as it always will be, since they have conserved more than 95 percent of their land through the Montana Land Reliance.

We rode horses, from which, amazingly, I didn't fall; fished the Yellowstone River; ate elk harvested by our hosts; and wondered at the drought that produced drier conditions than a neighbor had seen in fifty years. We spent our time looking for beauty, and beauty was on display in abundance.

But, as is so often the case, books open up another world entirely.

I read *Sapphira* (one of Cather's weaker books) and was halfway through both the trip and *The Corrections* (highly entertaining) but still felt something missing. Greg and Anne introduced us to a first-rate independent bookstore, Country Bookshelf, in Bozeman. While Dorothy read to Juliana, I explored the well-organized and well-stocked shelves.

I found Frances McCue's *The Car That Brought You Here Still Runs: Revisiting the Northwest Towns of Richard Hugo*, which, when coupled with Hugo's poems, brings to gray life another far-less beautiful Montana—struggling, left-behind, and more than a bit drunk and dirty.

McCue and photographer Mary Radlett visited many of the small towns Hugo used as "triggers" for his poetic and personal searchings. Most are in Montana, where Hugo lived towards the end of his life when he taught at the University of Montana in Missoula.

The book is hard to classify. It is part biography, part literary criticism, part travelogue, part memoir, but mostly a history of a number of damaged places occupied by damaged people. People who "washed up there" and stayed on, despite or perhaps because of the fact that whatever caused a town to be there in the first place (mining, train stops, etc.) disappeared a long time ago.

In the end, McCue's book is a form of literary investigation. She searches for the meaning of Hugo's poems in the places that inspired them. It results in a "close reading," not an academic literary analysis but something better. McCue writes that Hugo's "attention to the actual places could be scant, but Hugo's poems capture the torque between temperament and terrain that is so vital in any consideration of place." What a felicitous phrasing that is—"torque" is the perfect word, and McCue's explorations deepen our comprehension of Hugo's poems by exploring local history and local characters. So in the end, we get a powerful sense of what life is like in these struggling Montana towns—Dixon, St. Ignatius, Milltown, Walkerville, Philipsburg, Butte, Pony, Silver Star, and Fairfield.

McCue records the hidebound hostility of the old-timers towards newcomers. Sparing neither coast, signs in a Dixon bar that Hugo frequented argue that "My Montana has an east infection" and also "Save the Northwest: Spay and Neuter Californians." And she shows how Hugo's earthy, fishing-addicted, bar- and bourbon-crazed work inspired little affection, when it was noticed at all. Many residents of Dixon, for example, resented his depiction of their town, and others were displeased by his occasional traveling companion, the Native American author Jim Welch. The waitresses and, sadly, even the town librarian of Philipsburg, the locale of perhaps his greatest poem, "Degrees of Grey in Philipsburg," had not heard of Hugo or his poem and exhibited no eagerness to change that.

Dorothy, Juliana, and I did not get to these towns on this trip, but we'll try to if we travel to Montana again. In the meantime, we will remember the beauty of the Avis' ranch, and that we live in a nation that is home to many glorious saved places and a great many ruins as well.

August 2012

REGRET, "LOOKING BACK," AND DORIS GRUMBACH

I ENJOY CERTAIN books and creative nonfiction that are part memoir, part social commentary—they are what I call a "look back." They are not chronological accounts of a full life but consist instead of a more poetic compilation of regrets, nostalgia, and reflections on the passing of time. Written late in life, they have a bittersweet feel and are full of thoughts that only come together when the author has had ample time to reflect. They exist in a very different universe from bestsellers such as *A Million Little Pieces* and the many other sensationalist, ballistic memoirs that are an unhappy and untrustworthy cross between fact and fiction.

If there is one abiding emotion or thought associated with this "look back" it is regret. As the poet Hayden Carruth wrote, "Regret, acknowledged or not, is the inevitable and in some sense necessary context—the bedrock—of all human thought and activity. Intellectually speaking, it is the ground we stand on."

Of course there are many different forms of regret, and not all of them are entirely negative, even though all have to do with a form of sadness. Perhaps the most common form of regret as we age is that time is running out, which implies, rather happily, that you would rather it did not. And coming to terms with death and its proximity is often a large part of the enterprise. Note here Julian Barnes' compelling memoir, *Nothing to Be Frightened Of*, which contains a beautiful line, which summarizes my own spiritual state: "I don't believe in God, but I miss him."

Most authors writing in this vein have gotten to the point where what there is seems inferior to what there was, to what has passed. Also essential to the success of such books is that the author is to a considerable degree past affectation and pretense. There can be no "puffing up" of the self—it is too late for that, and besides it doesn't really matter, does it?

My favorite writer in this realm is Doris Grumbach. Her work is difficult to classify. She has written seven novels and six memoirs that are in this amorphous area of diary, commonplace book, cultural criticism, and spiritual exploration. Her own long life is complex. Born in 1918, she married Leonard Grumbach in 1941. They raised four daughters before their divorce in 1971. The rest of her years have been spent with her "life partner," Sybil Pike. Grumbach has taught literature at American University, written columns for the *New York Times Book Review* and the *New Republic*, run two used bookstores, and been a commentator for National Public Radio's *Morning Edition*. Now ninety three, she resides in Sargentville, Maine, an area of five square miles with a year-round population of about seventy five.

Many critics do not know what to make of her. Her books are not large sellers and are no longer widely reviewed, yet she must have a devoted following, as most are still in print. In bookstores you can find her books in fiction, religion, memoir, or in another amorphous "category"—gay and lesbian writers.

Whatever category she belongs in, she is good company. And her work, fiction and nonfiction, takes a close look at the particulars of individual lives, usually from the perspective of "looking back." In the main, she allows her readers to draw the larger conclusions.

Her novels are mostly re-imaginings of the lives of real people—Sylvia Plath (*The Magician's Girl*, 1987), Marilyn Monroe (*The Missing Person*, 1981) and Edward and Marian MacDowell (*Chamber Music*, 1979). In *Chamber Music*, Caroline Maclaren "looks back" from ninety at a life spent in a conventional, loveless marriage. The critic John Leonard wrote of the novel that "it is as if Willa Cather decided to tell the whole truth." In depicting the costs of such arrangements, Grumbach is never strident, although some of the revelations of her characters' pasts are gruesome. Lives spent in the wrong pairing are usually painful, and Caroline is allowed only a brief glimmer of what life could have been. She shares love with her husband's caregiver, Anna, but it is only a brief respite. She has been a nearly lifelong prisoner in a cage made by other hands. As one reviewer has observed, Grumbach may not be a political novelist, but her stories bring to life why politics matters.

It is her memoirs that appeal most to me: *Coming into the End Zone* (1991), *Extra Innings* (1993), *Fifty Days of Solitude* (1994), *Life in a Day* (1996), *The Presence of Absence: On Prayers and Epiphany* (1998), and *The Pleasure of Their Company* (2001). A recent essay, "The View from 90," published in the Spring 2011 edition of the *American Scholar*, is reported to be part of a larger memoir to be titled *Downhill Almost All the Way*.

If you are interested in Grumbach's writing, I suggest starting with *Fifty Days of Solitude*. It is a short book and contains all the hallmarks of Grumbach's nonfiction. Or start with "The View from 90," which you can download.

In "The View from 90," she provides wonderful, telling anecdotes to illustrate her points, as well as her usual handful of magnificent quotations. She must keep great notes from her reading as her writing is full of spot-on quotes that always cause me to reach for pen and paper.

Here, a decade after her last memoir, she is even more eager to repudiate the sentimental view of aging characterized by that misleading expression "the golden years." She notes how her youthful writings are sprinkled with exclamation points and that with age that form of punctuation went out, as did the fervor. "The old are pessimists," she states, "because they cannot conjure up the energy for optimism." She tells the story of Somerset Maugham, who, when asked to lecture on the virtues of being old, rose "to the podium, stared at the audience for a few seconds, said 'I cannot think of one,' and left the platform."

She does not sentimentalize the past either, referring to her childhood as having been lived in "those wretched years" between the two world wars. But she misses a great deal that is no more and provides many examples to do with writing—fountain pens, airmail paper, lined pads, and manual typewriters. She bemoans the fact that "the lovely Blackwing 602 soft-lead pencil with a removable and reversible eraser is nowhere to be found." (I remember that pencil well, as it was my mother's favorite.)

She notes her disdain for malls and her fond memories of butcher shops, dry goods stores, greengrocers, and hatters. She expresses her affection for Brownie cameras and that she prefers black and white photographs to colored ones, which "have a kind of violence, an excess, what I see as overemphasis." She notes that "Goethe called color 'the suffering of light.'" Lovely, that sentiment and quotation.

She wants to face things—squarely, no delusions. Solitude, "frequent journeys into her interior self," the time to think deeply about the important questions—these are her primary tools. About friendships, she quotes Proust, saying they are "a lie that seeks to make us believe that we are not irredeemably alone." In her interior quest she is not looking for the easy out, believing, for example, that faith in a life after death is "a sloppy consolation."

So once you reject such sloppy consolations, what is left?

Grumbach finds solace in ruins. "Why is this so? Ruins are not in themselves always beautiful. But like us they are the remains of what was once a more perfect whole. They have withstood the destructive forces of time. There is a certain rightness, an inevitability, about their decline. They are my fellow structures, my companions over time."

And there is much to be said for just keeping on, knowing what is asked of us. At the end of *The Presence of Absence*, she quotes these words from the Talmud:

"Look ahead

You are not expected to complete the task

Neither are you permitted to lay it down." *September 2012*

STRUGGLING IN THE SYSTEM AND WENDELL BERRY'S LONELY AGRARIAN VISION

PERHAPS THIS COLUMN would be better called "Readings and Reflections," as the two intersect for me as they do for most readers. That is particularly so with this edition, which addresses, among other matters, the diminished reach of mainstream politics; the paucity of great American political novels; Spielberg's film about Lincoln; and the long career of Wendell Berry, a wonderful American writer, activist, and farmer from our neighbor to the south, Kentucky.

I have spent my life working in the system. I do not regret that fact, but often wonder about the alternatives. I think about this more as it becomes clear that our political system is unable to tackle the most pressing problems that threaten our future.

I grew up in Washington, D.C., in the heady days of the civil rights movement and the Vietnam War protests. There was great conflict and debate on the big issues of the day. Young people were frustrated by the inability of our elders to use the resources of a booming economy to make more progress on issues of race and poverty. But, as a nation, we embarked on big programs, such as sending a man to the moon, and embraced big dreams. Emboldened by the seemingly infinite possibilities of the era, both Martin Luther King Jr. and President Johnson spoke of ending poverty in our lifetimes.

I absorbed all of this and it shaped me in fundamental ways. In 1968, when I was twelve years old, I was volunteering evenings in the headquarters of Senator Eugene McCarthy's quixotic campaign for the presidency.

I inhaled biographies of political figures, both well-known and more obscure. I believed then, and to a considerable extent still do, that real change in America is made by those who understand and work within the system. And I believed that the system could accommodate the dreams of all Americans and create the better world we saw as just around the corner.

Later I got a serious taste of life in electoral politics. In 1994, after twenty years of activism and eight years as a state legislator, I was the under-financed, long-shot Democratic nominee for governor of Massachusetts. Trounced by the highly popular Republican incumbent, I changed course and poured my energy into public education. That too is a bruising, highly factionalized field, where rancorous squabbling obscures the need to analyze and effectively implement policies that might significantly improve schools.

Over time I have grown more skeptical about what can happen within the system and more interested in the voices of those who have chosen to remain on the outside. Partly this is because big ideas seem to be a thing of the past in mainstream politics; in fact, even modestly aspirational public solutions have been hard to come by. Sadly, this has happened during a time in which many of our problems have grown so large that even the incremental approaches that appear beyond our reach are arguably delusional.

Increasingly I turn to what might be described as "public thinkers." I do this with some reluctance, as time spent in elected politics leaves me with a full understanding that actually getting things done in the public arena is far more challenging than talking, writing, or teaching about it. Advocates and critics are not required to work things out with others, to engage in the compromise and horse trading that allows you to actually get something accomplished in the real world.

As an aside, although there are many marvelous political biographies—Robert Caro's work on Robert Moses and Lyndon B. Johnson, for example—there is very little American fiction that truly illuminates the political process. Many believe that Robert Penn Warren's *All the King's Men* is our only great political novel, although Billy Lee Brammer's unfairly neglected novel about LBJ, *The Gay Place*, and some of Ward Just's work comes close. One of the many beauties of Steven Spielberg's film *Lincoln*, whose screenplay was adapted from Doris Kearns Goodwin's *Team of Rivals: The Political Genius of Abraham Lincoln*, is that it tells the story of a lofty political event—enactment of the Thirteenth Amendment to the U.S. Constitution—in part through the many unlofty actions, including various forms of bribery, that contributed to its passage. The film gives you Lincoln the dreamer and visionary, but also Lincoln the politician, willing to do what is necessary to get something important done.

But even having great respect for people who still fight the good fight "in the arena," the limited nature of mainstream public dialogue means that we desperately need outside voices, and places such as Antioch College, to raise the really big questions and to explore ideas for significant change—both of which our political structure seems hell-bent on avoiding. This is perhaps most true on environmental issues, where the requirements of electoral politics seem to dictate ignoring the increasingly substantial damage the way we live is doing to the long-term health of the planet.

It is likely that the greatest challenge of our time is to recognize that growth is a cause rather than an answer to many of our most significant problems. Growth in population, in consumer goods, in the size of houses are root causes of our downhill slide to self-destruction. If this is so, then it would be good if we paid more attention to Wendell Berry.

Berry has written more than fifty books, including novels, short stories, poetry, and essays on agriculture, religion, politics, and the human condition. He has done all this while still working a 125-acre farm in Lane's Landing, Kentucky. A political activist and lifelong member of the Baptist Church, Berry has received many honors and recently delivered the 2012 Jefferson Lecture for the National Endowment for the Humanities, a lecture described as "our nation's highest honor for distinguished intellectual achievement." Yet he and his ideas are unknown to a vast majority of his countrymen.

A FARM NEAR LEXINGTON, KENTUCKY, AROUND 1940
Library of Congress

Partly this is so because Berry is a regional writer, deeply bound to a few miles of both real and fictional land in Kentucky. Most of his novels and short stories are based in Port William, a fictional Kentucky community that is a fully developed world with its own town map and family trees that track its inhabitants from 1784 to the current day. These are sweet, slow-moving books.

His work as an author and an advocate is symbiotic. His writings honor his home ground and the lives of its inhabitants, and his political life is a fight for the future prospects of that land and its people.

His deepest belief is in small-scale farming and living. He has said that "local economies are being destroyed by the…displaced global economy, which has no respect for what works in a locality. The global economy is built on the principal that one place can be exploited, even destroyed, for the sake of another place."

Berry's Jeffersonian distrust of government can rankle, and, like many idealists, he can appear very naïve. He says change will come from the bottom up, one farm and community at a time, and is as cynical about large-scale, government-sponsored solutions as Tea Party activists.

In his Jefferson Lecture, published in book form as *It All Turns on Affection*, Berry traces the economic misfortune of his family and community to the actions of the American Tobacco Company and its president, James B. Duke. He endorses Wallace Stegner's separation of Americans into two groups—"boomers" and "stickers." Boomers are "those who pillage and run," whereas stickers are "those who settle, and love the life they have made and the place they have made it in."

"The boomer," Berry says, "is motivated by greed, the desire for money, property, and therefore power...stickers on the contrary are motivated by affection, by such love for a place and its life that they want to preserve it and remain in it." For Berry, everything ties to the land. And no subsequent action absolves a person of his responsibilities to respect it. So when he visits Duke University and comes upon a statue of its founder, the aforementioned James B. Duke, he draws a sharp distinction between his grandfather, ruined by the tobacco monopoly, and Duke, who profited from it.

"After my encounter with the statue, the story of my grandfather's 1906 tobacco crop slowly took on a new dimension and clarity in my mind," Berry says. "I still remembered my grandfather as himself, of course, but I began to think of him also as a kind of man standing in thematic opposition to a man of an entirely different kind. And I could see finally that between these two kinds there was a failure of imagination that was ruinous, that belongs indelibly to our history, and that has continued, growing worse, into our own time."

Berry's stubbornly agrarian vision is radical, populist, and deeply conservative. He is an heir to William Jennings Bryan and the Vanderbilt Agrarians who authored *I'll Take My Stand: The South and the Agrarian Tradition* in 1930. He and his brethren have been on the losing side of nearly every major political battle of the last two hundred years.

But that does not mean he has nothing to offer even those of us who have lived lives very far from his vision. His lecture notes that his father looked out at his land and felt he needed nothing more. How many of us have ever felt that way? Much of modern life is built upon engendering dissatisfaction with what we have and the desire to accumulate more and more of, well, something else that we do not have. In Berry's view, that leads exactly nowhere.

It is an unsettling vision that seeks to upend much on which we have built what we think of as civilization. Berry dislikes bigness and abhors our addiction to its pursuit through growth. Quoting E.M. Forster's novel *Howard's End* and its "manifesto against materialism," he writes: "It is the vice of a vulgar mind to be thrilled by bigness, to think that a thousand square miles are a thousand times more wonderful than one square mile…. That is not imagination. No, it kills it…. Your universities? Oh, yes, you have learned men who collect…facts, and facts, and empires of facts. But which of them will rekindle the light within?"

To Berry and Forster, "the light within" is affection. And for Berry, affection for the land is at the core, central to both culture and economy. He writes: "I am nominating economy for an equal standing among the arts and humanities. I mean, not economics, but economy, the making of the human household upon the earth; the arts of adapting kindly the many human households to the earth's many ecosystems and human neighborhoods. This is the economy that the most public and influential economists never talk about, the economy that is the primary vocation and responsibility of every one of us."

Does Berry really believe change will come from a grassroots movement built by "small is better" advocates? I doubt it. He has seen too much of life to give that much chance. I suspect that he sees some dramatic environmental calamity as the likely catalyst for change.

And in that he is not alone.

I write the end of this piece in my office on a cold gray Sunday. On the cover of today's *New York Times Sunday Week in Review* is an article by James Atlas titled "Is This the End?" Atlas contemplates Hurricane Sandy, not as the "storm of the century" but as a harbinger of things to come, and he prophesizes the eventual submergence of New York, "whether in 50 or 100 or 200 years." He notes that no civilization foresees its own decline and eventual disappearance. He appears to believe our own fate is sealed because "[our] species tends to see nature as something of a nuisance, a phenomenon to be outwitted."

Perhaps the calamity is not so close at hand; perhaps we can still create a better relationship with the land. But to get there, we will have to listen to outside voices such as Wendell Berry and change the way we think about many things, including words with weighty meaning—words such as "progress," "economics," "growth," "culture," civilization," and, yes, "affection."

October 2012

LOSS, GRIEF, AND SONALI DERANIYAGALA'S *WAVE*

In *How Literature Saved My Life*, David Shields writes, "I find books that simply allow us to escape existence a staggering waste of time (literature matters so much I can hardly stand it)."

As I sometimes read to distract myself, I do not agree with the first clause. But I do agree with the second: literature matters enormously.

Literature compels us to confront the precariousness of joy and contentment, even the blessedness of the absence of great pain. It urges, prods, implores, and even smacks us in the face not to take good fortune of any kind for granted. Grief is a considerable part of our lives and there is a reasonably large body of work that depicts what it means to try to cope in the aftermath of a tragic event. As students many of us were assigned *Death Be Not Proud*, John Gunther's portrait of his son Johnny's losing struggle with brain cancer. Joan Didion applies her clean, lucid prose to the deaths of her husband and daughter in *The Year of Magical Thinking* and *Blue Nights*. Donald Hall has written extensively in both poetry and prose of his awkward life after the passing of his wife. C.S. Lewis married at fifty eight; four years later his unexpected happiness was taken from him when his wife died of cancer. Reeling, Lewis authored *A Grief Observed*, noting that with such a loss the "first plunge of the knife into the flesh is felt again and again."

The plunge of the knife is given graphic examination in Sonali Deraniyagala's *Wave*. Deraniyagala was vacationing at a beach resort in her native Sri Lanka at the time of the December 2004 tsunami that killed more than 230,000 people. Looking out her hotel window, she saw the ocean approaching and yelled "menacingly" at her husband to join her. Not knowing exactly what they were seeing but somehow realizing what it meant, they were able to grab their two young sons and get themselves out to the hotel parking lot and into a Jeep in which they attempted to outrun the wave. They could not. Engulfed by the onrushing water, the Jeep tipped over. Her husband and two sons were swept away and drowned. By some miracle, Deraniyagala survived by hanging onto a tree limb. She spends most of the next half decade wishing she had died.

Wave examines her grief at a granular level. She is in such pain that nothing else matters and she is sure it never will. But after some time, the memories of her prior happiness begin to matter, if only because it helps her to hold on to her loved ones. But Deraniyagala never lets you think there is an end to the pain and certainly not a larger purpose to her suffering. *Wave* is not a self-help book or a book of spiritual discovery.

Deraniyagala is not trying to show us how she recovered. She clearly does not believe that "recovery," whatever that might mean, is possible.

She is also not interested in the larger issues. Despite its title, *Wave* is not about the tsunami, nor is it about the suffering of other people. Deraniyagala can hardly stand to be around other people and feels intense anger, especially at people she believes could not fathom what she is experiencing. Asked by a woman seated next to her on a plane whether she has a family, she writes, "Oh shut up you nosy cow, I think. You will probably faint if I tell you. You'll have to pull down your oxygen mask."

Pulling down the oxygen mask or even fainting would be a natural reaction, so why read a book such as *Wave*? That is a difficult question to answer. I have led a privileged life but am experienced enough not to need additional reasons to go home and hug my loved ones and feel immensely grateful that they are there to be hugged. I know that a life unmarred by real tragedy is a lucky life.

A friend said she would never read such a book because "when I am immersed in darker things it is harder for me choose happiness." But it is not so for me. *Wave* pained me, but it pained me in a way that left me more, rather than less, life embracive.

Of course loss and joy are intimately connected. Shakespeare is believed to have remarked that all literature is about loss. Novelist Rick Bass used to fight that notion, "preferring to write out of joy… bearing witness to the things I love during this brief life—it took me a while to realize that even the act of celebrating is an acknowledgment of loss for it is the temporal nature of celebration—the awareness that a thing has not always been one certain way before, and may not always be thereafter—which most sharpens the poet's and the reader's senses. Celebration and loss are shadows of one another in literature."

March 2013

THE DISCOVERY OF PATRICK O'BRIAN

WRITING THAT BREAKS new ground often has trouble reaching a large readership, but momentum builds as these works find advocates among bookish people. For the past few years the hottest such books have been Edward St. Aubyn's spectacularly maudlin novels about the hideous parenting and drug-addled youth of British aristocrat Patrick Melrose. As I write today, St. Aubyn is being supplanted by the similarly autobiographical but remarkably un-histrionic Norwegian author, Karl Ove Knausgaard, two volumes of whose semi-fictional magnum opus have been published in America as *My Struggle*.

In the early 1990s, if you were asked in an urgent tone, "Are you reading them?" it was very likely that the "them" referred to the novels of Patrick O'Brian.

The story of O'Brian's novels' emergence as literary favorites is almost as spectacular as the novels themselves. The series was originally published in the United States by Lippincott in 1969, but poor sales caused the publisher to drop the series in 1973, after only the third installment. The novels continued to be published in Great Britain, receiving modest attention and commercial success. Authors of historical fiction often struggle to find an audience, and despite his mastery of the form, O'Brian was no exception. One British critic, Peter Wishart, wrote that "The relative neglect of Patrick O'Brian by both critics and the book-buying public is one of the literary wonders of the age. It is as baffling as the Inca inability to invent the wheel; or conversely, it is as baffling as the Inca ability to possess an ordered, sophisticated society without the wheel."

Finally in 1990, W. W. Norton & Company returned O'Brian to print in America, publishing the twelfth installment, *The Letter of Marque*, in hardback and its predecessors in uniform paperback editions. By this time, a small coterie of loyal and influential readers had become aggressive proselytizers and, in retrospect, O'Brian's eventual success seems inevitable. But a jolt of some kind was required. That jolt was provided by Richard Snow, Editor of *American Heritage*, whose January 1991 front-page article in the *New York Times Book Review* was entitled "An Author I'd Walk the Plank For." Snow seemed to realize he had just one chance to make his case and pulled no punches, calling O'Brian's series "the best historical novels ever written." He concluded, "On every page O'Brian reminds us with subtle artistry of the most important of all historical lessons: that times change but people don't, that the griefs and follies and victories of the men and women who were here before us are in fact the maps of our own lives."

Snow's essay inspired me to read the first novel, *Master and Commander*, and I was immediately hooked. I read the next eleven already published volumes in a few months and eagerly awaited the arrival of each new installment. The twenty-volume series has given me as much pleasure as any books I have read.

O'Brian's books revolve around the exploits of the British navy during the Napoleonic wars, the same terrain as C.S. Forester's Horatio

"FIGHT OF THE BRITISH THIRD RATE 74-GUN SHIP-OF-THE-LINE HMS TREMENDOUS (IN THE FOREGROUND) AND HMS HINDOSTAN AGAINST THE FRENCH FRIGATE LA CANONNIÈRE, 21 APRIL 1806."
Museum of the History of France

Hornblower novels for younger readers. The action, as many early reviewers pointed out in a critical way, is rather limited and not at all the main draw. The novels are about character and how character interacts with society and culture, in this case mostly the characters of ship captain Jack Aubrey and ship physician Stephen Maturin and how they relate to each other and their compatriots in the petri-dish-like world of a British frigate, the *Surprise*. Aubrey is a creative sailor, combatant, and leader much more assured at sea than on land. Maturin is a doctor, spy, and leading naturalist who searches for new species of bird and beetle as the *Surprise* pursues the French to all corners of the globe.

And there is something else—an excited embrace of life's possibilities as exhibited by adventuresome and curious folk in the early nineteenth century, barely two hundred years past, but worlds away from how we live today. This change in zeitgeist is described well by Anthony Lane in his review of the enjoyable 2003 film *Master and Commander: The Far Side of the World*, comprised of events in several of the novels. Lane writes that "what the novels leave us with, and what emerges more fitfully from this film, as if in shafts of sunlight, is the growing realization that, although our existence is indisputably safer, softer, cleaner, and more dependable than the lives of Captain Aubrey and his men, theirs were in some immeasurable ways better—richer in possibility, and more entrancing to the eye and the spirit alike. As Stephen said of the Iliad, 'The book is full of death, but oh so living.' Just so: if you died on board the *Surprise*, it would not be for want of having lived."

Who was the man who created these wonderful books? Perhaps above all he was hard working, publishing many other novels, stories, biographies (including one of Pablo Picasso), and translations (including the popular prison escape memoir *Papillion*), in addition to the Aubrey/Maturin series. And he was an indefatigable researcher, steeped in early nineteenth century life on the seas and on land, a particular expert in the arcane details of scientific explorations and naval battles. He was also a private man who countenanced few personal questions from interviewers, and a bit of a recluse who made his home in Collioure, a small Catalan port in southern France. He was also a fibber.

O'Brian manufactured critical parts of his biography. He said that he was born and raised in Ireland, but he was born Richard Patrick Russ to middle-class parents in England. He changed his name by "deed poll" from Russ to O'Brian in 1945, at the time of his second marriage. For most of his life, he failed to acknowledge his siblings as well as his first marriage and two children.

Whether these personal limitations should matter to us is a subject for legitimate debate. It is sufficient here to note that O'Brian's misstatements of fact went unquestioned for the most part until Dean King, the author of several books about the Aubrey/Maturin novels, started delving into the historical record, eventually publishing *Patrick O'Brian: A Life Revealed* in 2000, a few months after O'Brian's death at eighty-six. This biography shows us how O'Brian kept plugging away. He believed in his work and withstood years of disappointment until, well past seventy years of age, he received the accolades and financial rewards that his hard work and talent should have afforded him long before. But O'Brian's story is also sad. He so isolated himself from many relationships, with his siblings and his own son, that his life feels more of a retreat than his admirers might have hoped.

An artist such as O'Brian leaves readers the legacy of his books, not his flawed personal conduct. So, as time and age have dimmed my memory, I will soon return to his novels. Once again I will be grateful for this wonderful gift of a fully drawn portrait of a world very different from my own, peopled by characters it would have been good to know, and graced with vivid accounts of explorations that take me back to the time, not that long ago, when our kind was still cataloging the discovery of unknown species. For a few happy months at least, these twenty volumes will distract me from the knowledge that just two hundred years later, our energies are devoted to documenting the extinction of many of those same species, doomed by human activity with its origins in an industrial age, which at the time of Aubrey and Maturin was visible on the horizon, but was still far less menacing than the outlines of an approaching French man-of-war, under sail, preparing for action.

February 2014

"DOWN THESE MEAN STREETS A MAN MUST GO"— RAYMOND CHANDLER

THERE ARE SOME things you have to look away from if you are going to make it through the day and stay sane. The human population explosion and the resulting extinction crisis among other species is one such topic for me.

But just because there are things I have to turn away from does not mean I want to avoid reality entirely, just that part of reality that seems too difficult to bear. For comfort I don't turn to "cheery" music or stories. Attempts at glossing things over exacerbate rather than relieve a sour mood. Instead, I find that certain kinds of dark books make me feel better, perhaps because they acknowledge life's myriad challenges, or perhaps because they remind me how much worse things can get.

Of course what kind of dark books hit home has a great deal to do with your life experience and particular way of looking at the world. I am attracted to stories—often crime novels—in which the main character exhibits well-earned world weariness but still struggles to make a difference.

For that reason and because of the magical quality of his writing, Raymond Chandler is one of my favorite writers. He wrote twenty-four short stories and seven novels. His later novels, especially *The Long Goodbye*, his masterpiece, are wonderful pain-filled searches for things to hold on to, love, or friendship. His protagonist,

Phillip Marlowe, is a loner who somehow maintains a certain wistful idealism. His life experience screams "give up," but he can't. In *The Long Goodbye* Marlowe says, "I hear voices crying in the night and I go see what's the matter."

In his essay "The Simple Art of Murder," Chandler writes that his protagonist is in search of redemption in a savage world. In his fictional world, "down these mean streets a man must go who is not himself mean, who is neither tarnished nor afraid.... The detective in this kind of story must be a complete man and a common man and yet an unusual man. He must be, to use a rather weathered phrase, a man of honor—by instinct, by inevitability, without thought of it, and certainly without saying it.... He is a lonely man.... He has a range of awareness that startles you, but it belongs to him by right, because it belongs to the world he lives in. If there were enough like him, the world would be a very safe place to live in, without becoming too dull to be worth living in."

Of course this sense of obligation to respond to nighttime cries is a heavy burden. And late in his career, his own life in shambles, Chandler seemed willing to let Marlowe cast it aside. In a draft of the last novel, *Playback*, Marlowe says, "Give up? Sure I give up. I'm in the wrong business. I ought to have given up before I started.... The hell with it." But Chandler eliminated the passage in the final version.

And now Marlowe battles on one more time as the Irish novelist John Banville, writing as Benjamin Black, has just published a new Marlowe novel, *The Black-Eyed Blonde*. Banville gets the essential aspects of Marlowe and his world right. His Marlowe knows that he is "a pushover" and understands what that portends. "I thought there wasn't much more damage that could be done to me that hadn't already been done. You get hardened by life knocking away at you since you were old enough to feel heart-sore, but then comes a knock that's bigger than anything you've experienced so far, and you realize just how soft you are, just how soft you'll always be."

Chandler's own life was pretty dreary. Before becoming a writer, he worked in the oil business, but he drank too much and was fired. Socially awkward and dominated by his mother, Chandler waited for her death to marry Cissy Pascal, a twice-divorced woman eighteen years his senior. They had no children, were easily bored and, to avoid staring at the same walls and views for too long, moved incessantly. They lived in more than thirty apartments and houses in their thirty years as a couple. After Cissy's death, Chandler, bereft, drank himself to death in five years' time.

But his dreary life did not keep him from writing magical prose. Interviewed in the December 15, 2013 *New York Times Book Review*, crime novelist Michael Connelly said that he would "like to ask Raymond Chandler about chapter 13 of *The Little Sister*. It describes a drive around 1940s Los Angeles, and it still holds up as a description of the city right now. Beautiful. I'd ask him how he pulled that off. And I'd tell him that that short chapter of his was what made me want to become a writer. I'd also ask him whether it takes a tortured life to produce something like that. I'd say, Ray, can a writer be happy and still be good at it?"

I do not know the answer to that. But perhaps fathoming how difficult it is to craft a decent life in a world that seems even madder today than it was in Chandler's day will help us better understand why we cannot get our act together to stop destroying the planet we live on. And we should also appreciate the art that Chandler made from his struggles. As A.O. Scott wrote in a recent film review in the *New York Times*, "We are, as a species, ridiculous: vain, ugly, selfish and self-deluding. But somehow, some of our attempts to take stock of this condition—our songs and stories and moving pictures, old and new—manage to be beautiful, even sublime."

March 2014

GIVING UP ON THE DREAM OF SUCCESS—
JIM HARRISON AND JIM GAVIN

FICTION REVEALS MORE than any other genre. I especially appreciate characters, about my age, who are seeking to understand what has happened to them, their world—to fathom the unlikely arc of their lives. Jim Harrison has offered me many such characters, and now he's added Clive, a sixty-year-old art history professor and the central character in the novella *The Land of Unlikeness* from the 2012 collection, *The River Swimmer*.

Clive has returned home to northern Michigan from New York City to examine his life after career, marital, and parental disappointments. The novella covers two weeks of his stumbling around, often inebriated, awkwardly interacting with a woman he was obsessed with in high school and his mother, who, although she cannot see well, glories in bird watching.

Unexpectedly and not in any straight line, Clive begins to regain a sense of what matters. He connects with the natural world again, to the sights, the smells, the memories, and the foods that signify he is home again. "It was Ralph's homemade pickled bologna, scarcely Proust's Madeline but then he was scarcely Proust. The odor of his childhood treat swept him precipitously back to his childhood, sitting in the rowboat fishing for bluegills with his dad and eating sharp cheddar and pickled bologna with saltines." And most importantly he connects again to what he first loved about art—doing it rather than studying, writing, lecturing, or appraising it. He orders new paints and brushes and gets to work.

He does not know it but he is being healed, in part by the physicality in his regained life—sex, awkward and clumsy as it may be, food, and work. He is seeing and feeling again, pushing against the many shackles that bound him.

And then one morning he is free. He has woken up having "lost his sense of self importance."

It is a lovely moment and it fuels Clive's journey to more. He reconnects with his estranged daughter, and they take a camping trip together. The novella ends with another simple, quiet moment as Clive awakens to see his daughter sitting by a campfire reading. "Behind Sabrina there was a shade of green on a moss-colored log he had never seen before…. He had had his dream of the world's idea of success but it was surprisingly easy to give up for his first love."

Fiction also offers a remarkable window on the times in which we live, which, as they change, leave many of us seriously out-of-step with what is happening around us.

We now live in the late early years of American decline. The spirit of these times is astronomically different than the years of American triumph in which I grew up, just half a century ago. Yes, even during the boom years, fiction writers documented the underside of American ascendancy, reminding us that not everyone shared in the good times. And writers such as Ross Macdonald showed how poverty and failure can be even harder to bear amidst all the glamour, wealth, and bright sun of Southern California. But deep in our bones, we knew the American story was one of constant rise, hard-charging forward movement that sooner or later was going to carry most of us on to better lives.

Jim Harrison and his character, Clive, come from that heady time. Clive, like most educated, ambitious, and upwardly mobile men, wrestles with the many choices offered by a prosperous nation. Other people, women and minorities, fought to get into that world of choice and privilege, and that produced much of the societal conflict of those years.

Now the path upward is clogged, perhaps especially for men. Most people are stuck where they are or are on the way down, rather than up, the economic ladder. This drama is playing out extensively in middle-class America, with profound effects on our national identity.

John Updike's subject was middle-class life. "I like middles. It is in the middles that extremes clash, where ambiguity restlessly rules," he wrote. If you look at the middle class of Updike's time and compare it to the middle class of today, the differences are vast. Rabbit Angstrom was an unsettled, often confused character. But central to Rabbit's life and world vision was the assumption that he and his generation would be better off than their predecessors.

No one presumes that anymore in America, and fiction writers are documenting the effect of this change in perspective on individual psyches. In Jim Gavin's *Middle Men,* there is an overwhelming sense of being trapped. The men it portrays may have dreams, but they do not really think they are going to be realized, even if they have occasional glimmers of hope. They have talent but not enough, and not that much ambition either. Whether they are salesmen, basketball players, plumbers, stand-up comedians, or screenwriters, they are never close enough to success to know what it would feel like. What they do feel is a certain numbness and the emptiness and drabness of their semi-suburban, semi-industrial surroundings. They are not modern Willy Lomans, as they are not that desperate, angry, or bitter. Instead they seem on the way to being almost "beyond dreams," although they are not sure what that really means.

The characters in *Middle Men* are splashing around in a stagnant pool, and lack the language to describe their condition. Our collective situation as a nation is very similar. We are struggling with how and what to think of ourselves in these first decades after the American century. It is a clumsy, awkward process made more difficult because so much of the national dialogue, especially the "it is still morning in America" mantra of our political leaders, refuses to acknowledge that we are in decline.

Such denial is not an option for the characters in *Middle Men*. They do not delude themselves that what has been lost—that pulsing, driving energy—can be regained. In their American moment, what counts is to gain a sense of balance and an understanding of what is possible given the new limitations. Clive's discovery of how important it is to define his own vision of success apart from more worldly aspirations is what beckons. Now that "the world's idea of success" is more difficult to obtain, the need to find a different measure of success is a journey few can avoid. The poetry of discovering that new shade of green is the language that we need, both as individuals and as a nation.

June 2013

"A BRIEF FOR THE DEFENSE"—
THE POETRY OF JACK GILBERT

THE POET Jack Gilbert died last year at eighty-seven. He was not famous, although he had a brief time of minor fame after his first book of poems won the Yale Prize and was nominated for the Pulitzer. He spoke about that time in his interview with the *Paris Review*: "I enjoyed those six months of being famous. Fame is a lot of fun, but it's not interesting. I loved being noticed and praised, even the banquets. But they didn't have anything that I wanted. After about six months, I found it boring. There were so many things to do, to live. I didn't want to be praised all the time—I liked the idea, but I didn't invest much in it."

How lovely that is—"But they didn't have anything that I wanted." As is his embrace of all that there is "to do." After his short stint of fame, he pretty much withdrew from society, with all its encumbrances, distractions, and demands. He wrote little and lived much; it took him twenty years to publish a second book. His *Collected Poems*, published in 2012, is slightly over four hundred pages.

Gilbert was born and raised in Pittsburgh and his affection for that city, where I also lived, is what first attracted me to his work. He wrote often of this bruised and resilient place. In 2006 the Pond Road Press published a collection of these poems, *Tough Heaven: Poems of Pittsburgh*. Gilbert's Pittsburgh poems are often set in romantic European cities. In "Trying to Have Something Left Over," the speaker is taking care of his Danish lover's baby:

> *Changing him and making him laugh.*
> *I would say Pittsburgh softly each time before*
> *throwing him up. Whisper Pittsburgh with*
> *my mouth against his tiny ear and throw*
> *him higher. Pittsburgh and happiness high up.*
> *The only way to leave even the smallest trace.*
> *So all his life her son would feel gladness*
> *unaccountably when anyone spoke of the ruined*
> *city of steel in America. Each time almost*
> *remembering something maybe important that got lost.*

After graduating from the University of Pittsburgh, Gilbert moved to San Francisco where he befriended Allen Ginsberg and other Beats, but he did not belong to a particular circle of poets. He spent many years in Denmark, Greece, Paris, and England, many of these with his first wife, the poet Linda Gregg. When he married a second time, to the sculptor Michiko Nogami, he moved to Japan, where he lived and worked until Nogami died of cancer in 1982.

Gilbert knew pain and anguish, and writes of it well. His third book, *The Great Fires: Poems 1982–1992* contains many grief-ridden poems about Nogami's death. Gilbert saw sadness and pain as intimately, inseparably, connected to life's better moments. His poems are filled with seeming dichotomies. In "All the Way from There to Here" he writes:

> *What I remember best of the four years of watching*
> *in Greece and Denmark and London and Greece is Linda*
> *making lunch. Her blondeness and ivory coming up*
> *out of the blue Aegean. Linda walking with me daily*
> *across the island from Monolithos to Thira and back.*
> *That's what I remember most of death:*
> *The gentleness of us in that bare Greek Eden,*
> *The beauty as the marriage steadily failed.*

Yet as aware as he is of the dark, he is overwhelmed by how much light somehow finds its way in. Gilbert's poems convey sadness for what has been taken, but a stubborn appreciation for having once had those things and anticipation for what else is still to come, which together, for him, is sufficient compensation. It is this worldly knowing and emphatically not Pollyannaish optimism that makes his poetry so important.

All of us have to wrestle with the pain of the world and what to make of it. Even those who lead lives unmarred by significant tragedy, such as the early death of a spouse, have to deal with multiple disappointments. Adam Begley's new biography of John Updike is a good reminder that even blessed lives are full of struggle. I think of this quality of Gilbert's poems the way the Irish writer Frank O'Connor wrote of Mozart's music: "It is a way of seeing things which revokes the tragic attitude without turning into comedy, which says, not 'Life is beautiful but so sad' but 'Life is sad but so beautiful.'"

The Lost Hotels of Paris

The Lord gives everything and charges
by taking it back. What a bargain.
Like being young for a while. We are
allowed to visit the hearts of women,
to go into their bodies so we feel
no longer alone. We are permitted
romantic love with its bounty and half-life
of two years. It is right to mourn
for the small hotels of Paris that used to be
when we used to be. My mansard looking
down on Notre Dame every morning is gone,
and me listening to the bell at night.
Venice is no more. The best Greek islands
have drowned in acceleration. But it's the having
not the keeping that is the treasure.
Ginsberg came to my house one afternoon
and said he was giving up poetry
because it told lies, that language distorts.
I agreed, but asked what we have

that gets it right even that much.
We look up at the stars and they are
not there. We see the memory
of when they were, once upon a time.
And that too is more than enough.

Is it? Gilbert is almost convincing. He has taken on a mission to help us doubters believe, if not in God, at least in life. His poems often seem the work of a poet playing the role of a lawyer defending whoever designed this world. Like Baroque sacred music, Gilbert's poems celebrate the beauty of that design to all who will listen.

We need voices such as Gilbert's to balance the countless others who have drawn a different conclusion from the same evidence.

His writing, and, even more, his wondrously productive, happy life serves as an eloquent "Brief for the Defense," the title of one of his best poems.

A Brief for the Defense

Sorrow everywhere. Slaughter everywhere. If babies
are not starving someplace, they are starving
somewhere else. With flies in their nostrils.
But we enjoy our lives because that's what God wants.
Otherwise the mornings before summer dawn would not
be made so fine. The Bengal tiger would not
be fashioned so miraculously well. The poor women

*at the fountain are laughing together between
the suffering they have known and the awfulness
in their future, smiling and laughing while somebody
in the village is very sick. There is laughter
every day in the terrible streets of Calcutta,
and the women laugh in the cages of Bombay.
If we deny our happiness, resist our satisfaction,
we lessen the importance of their deprivation.
We must risk delight. We can do without pleasure,
but not delight. Not enjoyment. We must have
the stubbornness to accept our gladness in the ruthless
furnace of this world. To make injustice the only
measure of our attention is to praise the Devil.
If the locomotive of the Lord runs us down,
we should give thanks that the end had magnitude.
We must admit there will be music despite everything.
We stand at the prow again of a small ship
anchored late at night in the tiny port
looking over to the sleeping island: the waterfront
is three shuttered cafés and one naked light burning.
To hear the faint sound of oars in the silence as a rowboat
comes slowly out and then goes back is truly worth
all the years of sorrow that are to come.*

April 2014

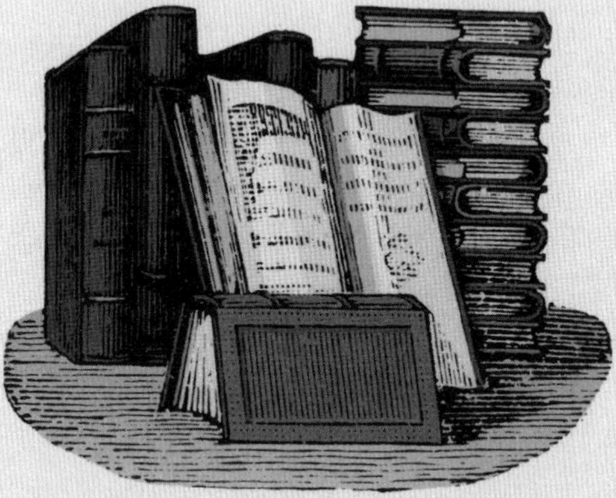

HISTORY

"LOOK INTO HIS BEAUTIFUL EYES"—ABRAHAM LINCOLN

WHAT FOLLOWS IS an expanded version of a talk I gave at the inaugural Dayton TEDx conference on November 15, 2013. At TEDx I had only nine minutes to explain why I love Abraham Lincoln and explore how Lincoln guided this nation through the worst crisis in our history—the Civil War—and how he resolved our most intractable problem and great national sin—slavery.

I ask the audience to reflect on how much most Americans know about Lincoln. We know that Lincoln is remembered. He is the subject of more than sixteen thousand books and recently Stephen Spielberg made a pretty good film about him. And he is still taught, as much as any American history is taught, in our content-deprived schools.

And if you go looking for Lincoln, you will certainly find his image. You will see his face in the signs and advertisements of the innumerable companies named after him and you will see statues and plaques of him in our public parks and buildings.

You can see his visage as you pay for your coffee at Starbucks with a five-dollar bill, or when you stoop to pick up one of the more than 450 billion pennies that have been minted with his face on one side.

I asked the audience: "What does Lincoln mean to you?"

What Lincoln has meant to most Americans has changed a great deal over time.

In his own lifetime, Lincoln was subject to vicious ridicule, much of which was about how he looked and sounded.

He was tall—6 feet 4 inches, or seven feet with his stovepipe top hat, and he was ungainly, with overly long arms and large feet. He appeared as if he needed oiling. His clothes did not fit very well. And when he spoke, his audience needed a few moments to adjust to his high-pitched, rather unpleasant voice.

Nathaniel Hawthorne was not alone in thinking Lincoln "was about the homeliest man I ever saw."

As was his wont, Lincoln used humor to deal with his looks, saying that "common-looking people are the best in the world, which is the reason God made so many of them."

Since his assassination, Lincoln has been much loved, primarily as a common man who rose to leadership. As late as 1952, Hancock Insurance Company would issue advertisements with him slumped over a too-small chair with the caption, "He was everybody, grown a little taller."

Yet although he was born a "common man," Lincoln came to embody all that is best in us as Americans and thus became uniquely uncommon.

He and his greatness are so unlikely that he still seems to me to be something like a miracle.

ROOSEVELT READS

LIBRARY OF CONGRESS

Who was this man who made more of himself and gave more of himself than anyone I know of?

Lincoln was a mass of contradictions.

Sad and contemplative, he brooded and was given to bouts of depression. Yet he was also funny. He was a loner who loved company. And he could be good company—friendly, kind, generous, and interested in other people's lives and problems.

He was humble, but also very ambitious. He wanted to accomplish great things.

He was a visionary, but he was also a politician unafraid to use the tools of the trade. Spielberg's film does a good job showing Lincoln doling out patronage, doing whatever it took to pass the 13th amendment to the Constitution, abolishing slavery.

He was born in a log cabin, but he did not conform to what we expect from a frontiersman. He did not hunt or drink or hate Indians. And he made fun of his role in the short-lived Black Hawk War of 1832.

Raised in what he called an "unbroken forest," he was required to do hard labor every day. But learning and reading, not toiling in the fields, is what he loved. He read deeply, mainly the Bible and Shakespeare, what the historian Fred Kaplan, author of *Lincoln: The Biography of a Writer*, calls "wisdom literature."

Lincoln worked especially hard to excel at what he believed mattered most, which was writing. As he worked at his craft, his writings and speeches grew so persuasive that he changed the way

Americans thought about race, the Declaration of Independence, the Constitution, and the meaning of the Civil War. He wrote every word himself, painstakingly, dwelling on the rhythms, the sounds, the inferences, and subtle meanings.

And Lincoln grew. He grew from incredible suffering. He suffered so much that you wonder how he kept going.

He and his wife Mary Todd had a difficult marriage, and they endured terrible losses. Their son Eddie died in 1850 at age three from tuberculosis. And in 1862, the low point of the Civil War, the Lincolns lost the child they loved most, Willie, who died of fever at age twelve.

Lincoln wept and grieved and got up to read the telegrams listing the dead and wounded on the battlefields, and wept some more, and wrote personal notes to the mothers of the dead, and sat up alone at night, wondering what could possibly explain or justify all this suffering.

Although not a member of an organized church, Lincoln spent his life immersed in the Bible and was deeply spiritual. He thought about God and he struggled with his faith. He searched for answers, for glimmers of understanding.

And this is where the miracle of Lincoln explodes into the world.

The Emancipation Proclamation came from the pen of a man who no longer doubted what he was meant to do. And from that time forward his vision was so clear, so distilled, that his speeches were magnificently concise. The Gettysburg Address was only 272 words and lasted only two minutes; the Second Inaugural was 701 words and lasted only seven minutes.

Abraham Lincoln had arrived at a place of insight and conviction that few have ever reached. He had arrived there by embracing what Elmer Trueblood in his magnificent book on Lincoln's religious views calls a "theology of anguish."

And in so doing he found a way out of our great national nightmare—slavery. Lincoln faced twin obstacles to eliminating slavery—public opinion and the Constitution. To convince a reluctant country that slavery must go, he put its eradication in the context of the commonly accepted American destiny to both establish and refine democracy. He had to convince people that how the war turned out would determine whether "we shall nobly save or meanly lose the last best hope of earth"—American democracy, which had been bequeathed, in his beautiful phrase, to "an almost chosen people." And he had to convince himself, and his cabinet among others, that the war powers granted him by the Constitution allowed him to act.

By the end, reflecting on his suffering and that of his countrymen, Lincoln had come to see the war as a plague visited upon America by the Almighty as punishment for slavery and himself as an instrument of God's will, tasked with ensuring that something good came of these horrific calamities. Namely, that democracy would be saved and the sin of slavery would be forever purged from our land.

In his second inaugural, Lincoln was expected to be celebratory. The war was nearly over and victory was close at hand. But instead of claiming credit for the coming triumph, Lincoln made it clear that slavery and its continuance was not only the cause of the war but a national sin shared by both sides in the conflict:

> *Both read the same Bible and pray to the same God, and each invokes His aid against the other. It may seem strange that any men should dare to ask a just God's assistance in wringing their bread from the sweat of other men's faces, but let us judge not, that we be not judged. The prayers of both could not be answered. That of neither has been answered fully. The Almighty has His own purposes. "Woe unto the world because of offenses; for it must needs be that offenses come, but woe to that man by whom the offense cometh." If we shall suppose that American slavery is one of those offenses which, in the providence of God, must needs come, but which, having continued through His appointed time, He now wills to remove, and that He gives to both North and South this terrible war as the woe due to those by whom the offense came, shall we discern therein any departure from those divine attributes which the believers in a living God always ascribe to Him? Fondly do we hope, fervently do we pray, that this mighty scourge of war may speedily pass away. Yet, if God wills that it continue until all the wealth piled by the bondsman's two hundred and fifty years of unrequited toil shall be sunk, and until every drop of blood drawn with the lash shall be paid by another drawn with the sword, as was said three thousand years ago, so still it must be said "the judgments of the Lord are true and righteous altogether."*

Northerners were expecting to be congratulated for their persistence and resolve, not consigned a share of the blame, so these unexpected words left most listeners stunned and confused. But not Frederick Douglass. Douglass was gratified to hear such an extraordinary depiction of national and personal responsibility and marveled at how far his sometime antagonist and recent ally had come. In what is one of my favorite moments in American history, Douglass sought Lincoln out at the inaugural reception that night. As the historian David Blight recounts the scene:

At first denied entrance by two policemen, Douglass was admitted only when the President himself was notified. Weary of a lifetime of such racial rejections, Douglass was immediately set at ease by Lincoln's cordial greeting: "Here comes my friend Douglass." Lincoln asked Douglass what he thought of the day's speech. Douglass demurred, urging the President to attend to his host of visitors. But Lincoln insisted, telling his black guest: "There is no man in the country whose opinion I value more than yours." "Mr. Lincoln," replied the former slave, "that was a sacred effort."

Most Americans today do not comprehend that the Civil War did not have to end the way it did. The Union could easily have lost the war, leaving two nations, one with slavery and one without. If Lincoln had lost the election of 1864, the war would likely have been settled with both the Union and slavery still intact.

It was Abraham Lincoln who made it otherwise.

And we will never know what more Lincoln might have accomplished. In the second inaugural, he said the nation must press on with "malice towards none" and "charity for all" but also with a sense of "firmness in the right, as God gives us to see the right." And his vision of that "right" continued to grow. With but three days left to live, speaking to a crowd at the White House on April 11, 1865, Lincoln advocated voting rights for blacks who were educated or had served in the Union army. In the audience that day, as he had been at the second inaugural, Confederate zealot John Wilkes Booth knew full well what Lincoln's "firmness" meant for the old racial order and pledged "Now, by God, I'll put him through. That is the last speech he will ever make."

In wondering how to end my TEDx talk I realized that, for me, it is in Lincoln's face, especially near the end of his life, that we can see him clearest—we can see his suffering, his hard-earned wisdom, and his extraordinary decency.

In Maira Kalman's wonderful children's book *Looking at Lincoln*, a child goes in search of Old Abe. Beginning her search in library books she "gets lost in his unusual face," realizing that she "could look at him forever." After studying him a bit, she returns once again to his face. She ends the book by visiting the Lincoln Memorial, saying, "Look into his beautiful eyes. Just look."

October 2013

BOOKS ABOUT LINCOLN

MY MIND IS still on Lincoln. After all, this November marks the 150th anniversary of the Gettysburg Address. So this month I offer a few suggestions as to what to read if you want to spend some time with him.

There are more than sixteen thousand books written about Lincoln. I have only read about three dozen of these so certainly cannot claim that my favorites are the best available.

You might want to begin with an overview of the Civil War era, and in that category there is a clear first choice, James McPherson's *Battle Cry of Freedom*. McPherson's volume is one of the best books in the excellent *Oxford History of the United States*. McPherson undercuts many of the most persistent myths about the war, such as the view that Confederate generals were always superior to Union ones. And as his title indicates, he is not afraid to illuminate the moral dimensions of the conflict.

Many will want to start with a comprehensive biography of Lincoln. I have read many of the most respected one-volume biographies but do not have a clear first choice. David Donald, a professor of mine in college, is the author of the most praised one, *Lincoln*, which came out in 1995. It is certainly well-written and informative. As the historian Eric Foner notes, Donald avoids both hagiography and an overly critical slant. But I do not accept the platform on which his portrait is built, essentially that Lincoln was carried along by events more than he shaped them and that he lacked a larger purpose or moral center.

There are many other options. Benjamin Thomas' very readable biography came out in 1952 and was the standard for many decades. It covers the ground but feels a bit dated. Stephen Oates published *With Malice Towards None* in 1977 and offers a more current, workmanlike option. But I agree with Donald's assessment that Oates' portrait of Lincoln is a bit cold. I suppose if I had to recommend one, it would be Richard Carwardine's *Lincoln: A life of Purpose and Power*, which was published in 2006. Carwardine emphasizes Lincoln's political skills while not belittling his larger moral vision. But the book, which is only 321 pages long, feels a bit slight. One massive alternative, which sits on my bookshelf awaiting attention, is Michael Burlingame's recently finished million word, two-thousand page, two-volume treatise, although it is likely a bit much for those who are not deeply affected by the Lincoln bug.

My favorite Lincoln books are not biographies, or at least not traditional ones. Perhaps the best is Doris Kearns Goodwin's magnificent *Team of Rivals*. Its angle—that Lincoln's magnanimous nature was central to his success, allowing him to utilize the services of those who had previously been adversaries—is a wonderful organizing vehicle. Another is Fred Kaplan's *Lincoln: The Biography of a Writer*. Writing was Lincoln's form of thinking things through, and he worked at it painstakingly. Exploring him through that lens is very revealing.

Among the lesser known books, two that I particularly appreciate are focused on Lincoln's theology. Elton Trueblood's short but insightful *Abraham Lincoln: Theologian of American Anguish* has been recently reissued with the weaker title *Abraham Lincoln: Lessons in Spiritual Leadership*. A professor of religion at Earlham College, Trueblood believed the key to understanding Lincoln is coming to terms with his spirituality. As Gustav Niebuhr writes in the new preface, "No single writer can express Lincoln's greatness in its entirety, but when we deal seriously with his religious thinking we are getting close to the central mystery."

The first fifty pages of his short book are as good as any analysis of Lincoln that I know of. They exhibit none of the dryness or distance typical of academic writing, as Trueblood clearly reveres Lincoln and wants his reader to understand why. (That was the goal of my TEDx talk as well.) He wants us to share his belief that Lincoln was both good and great and that his greatness derived in part from his commitment to being good and to examining issues with the aid of his deep knowledge of the Bible.

Lincoln was not a simple man, and his religious thinking was hardly orthodox. He did not belong to a church or to a particular religious denomination. His spirituality is deeply connected to his suffering and his personal growth. Lincoln understood that, saying to a friend, "I have been driven many times to my knees by the overwhelming conviction that I had nowhere else to go." Trueblood's original title was apt—Lincoln's suffering and his search for understanding led him to develop a "theology of anguish." It was how he explained the world to himself, and it was how he explained the Civil War and all its horrors to his countrymen in his magnificent Old Testament-driven Second Inaugural Address.

That address is brilliantly examined in Ronald White's *Lincoln's Greatest Speech: The Second Inaugural.* White explores the unorthodox religious views that emerged from Lincoln's lifelong search as manifested in the 701-word address that serves as his "final statement," delivered only a few weeks before his death.

Another path to Lincoln that I recommend is through children's books. I often read a Lincoln book to my daughter Juliana. My eyes seldom remain dry. We especially like *Abe Lincoln Loved Animals* by Ellen Jackson. Unlike many of his frontier peers, Lincoln was upset from a very young age by cruelty to animals and never enjoyed hunting.

We also enjoy *Abe Lincoln's Hat* by Martha Brenner. This little book reminds us that Lincoln was an astounding seven feet tall when wearing his stovepipe top hat. And that he kept reminder notes tucked in the inside band.

And we return often to *Mr. Lincoln's Whiskers* by Karen Winnick. Winnick tells the story of eleven-year-old Grace Bedell, who wrote Lincoln a letter telling him he would look better with a beard. The fact that he replied to her, accepting her advice, and the kindly manner in which he did tells us more about Lincoln than many full-length biographies.

November 2013

THE OBSTINATE LEADERSHIP OF CHARLES DE GAULLE

THE BEST BOOK that I read in my usual holiday reading frenzy was Jonathan Fenby's biography of Charles De Gaulle, *The General: Charles De Gaulle and the France He Saved*. It is a long, dramatic, and beautifully told story of the least known and understood major figure from the allied side of World War II. De Gaulle is a fascinating and exceedingly annoying man. His personal qualities are so challenging that one wonders how he ever assumed a position of national leadership, and given his dictatorial mindset, how he managed to function at all in a democracy. And, yet, it is clear from Fenby's book that his victories and contributions significantly outweigh his failures.

Throughout De Gaulle's life it seemed more likely that he would end up in angry isolation than any form of triumph. Given to fits of pique, threats to resign, actual resignations, coldness, haughtiness, and inflexibility, De Gaulle triumphed through force of will, clear goal setting, and an overwhelming determination to endure and succeed. He believed in himself when no one else did and became, on more than one occasion, the pillar of strength his nation needed to survive. His story is a classic example of how a person's attributes battle with their deficits, and the outcome is determined as much by the needs of the situation as by any other factor.

The drama of the story is in good part how De Gaulle becomes France's necessary man. As France offered weak and disorganized resistance to the Nazi invasion in the spring of 1940, De Gaulle emerged from near obscurity as a resourceful general of an armored division, but he was not a major national figure. As the outcome of the invasion became clear, and other French "leaders" chose collaboration over resistance, De Gaulle left the continent to go to London to set up a "free" French government in exile, attempting to galvanize both French and other forces to support resistance to both the German occupation and the collaborationist government now ensconced in Vichy.

De Gaulle had some credentials. He was an early opponent of appeasement. He recognized the Nazi threat and warned against complacency and inaction. But it was his iron will more than his resume that drove his success. He had a nearly maniacal belief in the destiny of his nation and of himself, and he believed that these destinies were inextricably intertwined. And for a time they surely were. During World War II and for much of the time until his death in 1970, De Gaulle believed that he did not just represent France—he actually *was* France. In one of many scenes during the war in which his English allies were ready to abandon De Gaulle and search for virtually any other person they could anoint as head of the Free French, Britain's foreign secretary, Anthony Eden, said, "Do you know that, of all the European allies, you have caused us the most difficulties?"

De Gaulle replied, "I don't doubt that. France is a great power."

Of course it wasn't. Nor has France been a great power since World War II. But in many ways it still thinks of itself that way, for better or worse, in good part due to De Gaulle.

Sometimes it seems that there is a providential hand at work as nations or causes find the leader they need in times of crisis. Abraham Lincoln's election to the presidency in 1860 and the skills he displayed in winning the Civil War and ending slavery is one such moment. His rise to power, and to greatness, is such an unlikely tale that it is challenging to explain logically. And it is generally accepted that England found similar serendipity in the rise of Winston Churchill at the start of World War II. Churchill was often woefully out of place in times that did not require leadership of the most dramatic "our backs are against the wall" style. Most see FDR's depression-era and wartime leadership in much the same light. De Gaulle's is in many ways a similar story, only perhaps even more unlikely, as his skill set was so much more limited than the other three leaders.

The General is a story of a stubborn man and a declining nation, often at war with itself, full of tales of cowardice, especially as regards collaborators such as Petain, and also of great courage, shown by the resistance movement and often De Gaulle himself. It is a story of begrudgingly slow acceptance of new realties, such as the end of French rule in its colonies, and ugly resistance to these realities. As is depicted in the fictional thriller, *The Day of the*

Jackal, De Gaulle was the target of many assassination attempts by the Organization of the Secret Army, or OAS, and Frenchmen who refused to accept Algerian independence—which De Gaulle himself had engineered after coming to the realization that there was no other path.

Besides being a great story, *The General* has lessons for us in America at this time. Perhaps the most profound is about how factional, partisan bickering often prevented France from dealing with critical issues. De Gaulle insisted that he was above party and that a nation needs such leadership. Of course, when the status of being above the fray is located in only one person, there is the danger of dictatorship. But the perception that nations need leaders who rise above partisan squabbling has roots in our own origins as a nation.

In *Revolutionary Characters*, historian Gordon Wood explores why many of our country's founders believed it was essential for leaders to be "disinterested." By this they meant above the fray, above sectional, partisan, and especially pecuniary interest: the ability to put the nation's interests above all other considerations. The word "disinterested" has lost its power and this particular meaning and is now taken as being hardly different in meaning from "uninterested." But the word and the concept had powerful meaning as eighteenth-century American leaders contemplated the early effects of the age of commercialization. The founders believed that without disinterested leaders the nation would become "unvirtuous."

De Gaulle, too, abhorred the politicization of government and preferred the idea of an administration of leaders limited by neither party discipline nor electoral pressures. He resigned from the presidency in 1946 and only returned to power in 1958 because he believed he could govern with direct authority from the people and without factional or party pressures. For a while it worked and he guided the nation through thorny issues, and then it didn't, and he left power again, deeply worried about whether a factionalized government could chart a path to a better future.

Reading *The General* is a good reminder that when dealing with declining influence in the world, nations are far more susceptible than usual to nasty infighting, which deflects attention from the real problems they face. Especially in such times of dislocation, nations need leaders willing to speak honestly, to help their compatriots find a new way to think through where they fit in an increasingly complex, interconnected world.

The United States is now in a grumpy mood very similar to that of France through much of the mid-twentieth century. We also need to find our way to some form of post-partisan, above-the-fray problem solving. De Gaulle's personal example is in many ways a poor one, but his ability to get people to see threats they would rather ignore commands respect. Indeed, De Gaulle once said that his whole life consisted of getting people to do what they did not want to do.

January 2013

"AN ICE-AXE TO THE SOUL,"
THE BLOODLANDS OF EASTERN EUROPE

KAFKA WROTE, "A book must be an ice-axe to break the frozen seas inside our souls."

I have received many wonderful responses from Antiochians about this column, some with suggestions of books to read. Last month, Zee Gamson '59 wrote to me about how she had stayed up late into the night reading *Bloodlands: Europe Between Hitler and Stalin* by Timothy Snyder.

So I read *Bloodlands*, a book that epitomizes what it means to be an "ice-axe" to our souls and that provokes wonderment about the murderous nature of ideological fanaticism.

I have long been meaning to read more about the horrors that befell much of Eastern Europe during that time. I had been stirred by the historian Tony Judt's observations in *The Memory Chalet* about how the vast majority of left-leaning westerners of the 1960s were oblivious to the breathtaking cruelty of communism as practiced by the Soviet Union, as well as Mao and his brethren. I remember that I, too, owned a "Little Red Book" as a teenager, furious with my own country's misdeeds in Vietnam and Chile, but oblivious to anything that was happening in the overflowing prisons and graveyards of Beijing, Prague, Berlin, or Moscow.

Judt spent his life "on the left," but he grew to realize that in his rebellious youth, it was the student rebels in Poland, Hungary, and Czechoslovakia—not London, Paris, or New York—who were making the history that mattered most. Judt asks of his younger self, "What did we know of the courage it took to withstand weeks of interrogation in Warsaw prisons…for all our grandstanding theories of history we failed to notice one of its seminal turning points…. We protested the things we didn't like, and we were right to do so. In our own eyes at least, we were a revolutionary generation. Pity we missed the revolution."

I think about how important it is to search for the truth, and how difficult. So much can cloud our vision—our own personal histories, the limits of our knowledge and comprehension, the times in which we live, and the less-than-accurate lessons we have been taught about history from when we were first able to hear and read.

How easily history can be distorted, or ignored, is especially clear when we think of the Soviet Union. During the Cold War, for example, Americans were taught history from textbooks that warped our understanding of how World War II was won and the role played by our Russian allies. Reading many of these texts you would hardly have known that there was an Eastern Front, not to mention that it was the largest military engagement in the history of the world and resulted in thirty million deaths and was the primary cause of Hitler's defeat.

Who makes these decisions on what is taught and what is not? On what stories we are told and those that are kept hidden? It is easy to understand that it was difficult for many Americans to acknowledge the bravery and suffering of the people who had become our most feared enemy. But a more honest depiction of the past would have provided a clearer understanding of what we were up against in the Cold War and how best to deal with it.

If more scrupulous histories had depicted Russian bravery and sacrifice, it would also have chronicled enormous barbarity. For Americans and Europeans of the left, some of whom saw the Soviet Union as a beacon of hope, acknowledging that barbarity was difficult. That is unfortunate, for as *Bloodlands* reveals, the Soviet Union, both before and after the war, engaged in the systemic killing of millions through starvation, work camps, and executions, based on ethnicity, national origin, profession, and other characteristics now almost too obscure to fathom.

Bloodlands overpowers the reader with statistics of these grisly horrors, one after another, page after page. There is no escape for the reader as for decades there was no escape for Poles, Ukrainians, Germans, Russians, Belarusians, and Jews from every country, and so many others for whom their homelands would become the largest killing fields in history.

Snyder's extraordinary research from multiple sources in multiple languages pulls a complicated story into a cohesive whole that has heretofore mostly been told only in its horrific parts. Sometimes the piling up of statistics, and of bodies in mass graves, is more than the mind can absorb. The horror and the learning come through best in specifics. For example, because neither the Russians nor the

Germans honored codes for the treatment of prisoners of war, on any given day in the autumn of 1941 as many Soviet POWs died as did British and American POWs—during the entire war. Another example—as the war in the east went increasingly badly for the Germans, their dedication to "the final solution" increased. By 1941 the Nazis were killing all the Jews in communities they controlled. In the Babi Yar ravine in Kiev, they engaged in two days of continuous shooting, leaving more than 33,770 corpses. Eventually they would slaughter 2.5 million Jews in occupied Soviet territory.

In *Bloodlands* you read about individual people whose barbarity is beyond description. People such as Vasily Blokhin, the chief Soviet executioner in Kalinin, now Tver, a Russian town north of Moscow, who "wore a leather cap, apron, and long gloves to keep the blood and gore from himself and his uniform" and "shot, each night, about 250 men, one after another," reaching a total of more than 7,000 Polish prisoners executed in this one episode of mass killing alone. Because the extent of the depravity revealed in *Bloodlands* is so monumental in scope, Blokhin and the Kalinin massacre receive only a paragraph. Perhaps Snyder was sparing us from having to learn more gruesome details of Blokhin's technique, which earned him various "honors" from Stalin, including the Red Banner, and make him, according to other sources, "the most prolific official executioner in recorded world history." Such details jolt the reader to comprehension.

As Anne Applebaum, author of *Gulag: A History* and *Iron Curtain: The Crushing of Eastern Europe, 1944–1956*, observes in her article "The Worst of the Madness" in the November 11, 2010 *New York Review of Books*, *Bloodlands* records the misdeeds of two of the most murderous ideologies the world has ever seen—Soviet communist totalitarianism and German national socialism. Americans still lack the "jolt" of comprehension required to come to terms, if that is indeed possible. Applebaum notes that the Nobel Prize-winning Polish poet Czeslaw Milosz could never quite forgive Americans for this lack of awareness and explained that because of that, "the man of the East cannot take Americans seriously…their resultant lack of imagination is appalling."

What might true comprehension mean?

At the least, it requires us to ponder the dangers of ideology and to open our eyes as wide as possible.

Applebaum's own conclusions are worth quoting at length. She believes that "if we remember the twentieth century for what it actually was, and not for what we imagine it to have been, the misuse of history for national political purposes also becomes more difficult."

She also believes that this larger comprehension requires us to revise our view of World War II as "the good war," because although it is true that we fought successfully for human rights in Western Europe, "we ignored and then forgot what happened further east. As a result we liberated one half of Europe at the cost of enslaving the other half for 50 years…. That does not make us bad—there were limitations, reasons, legitimate explanations for what happened. But it does make us less exceptional. And it does make World War II less exceptional, more morally ambiguous, and thus more similar to the wars that followed."

Applebaum concludes that such a painful "reassessment… could finally cure us of that 'lack of imagination' that so appalled Czeslaw Milosz almost 60 years ago. When considered in isolation, Auschwitz can be easily compartmentalized…. But if Auschwitz was not the only mass atrocity, if mass murder was simultaneously taking place across a multinational landscape and with the support of many different kinds of people, then it is not so easy to compartmentalize or explain away."

That is the sort of revelation or "ice-axe to the soul" that kept Zee Gamson up through the night.

February 2013

IT DID NOT NEED TO BE THAT WAY—THE SERVICE OF WENDELL WILLKIE

I LEARNED A POWERFUL, if seemingly simple, lesson from a college history professor of mine, Bernard Bailyn. The lesson is that when you look back in history, what actually happened looks like it had to happen, that it was inevitable—but it wasn't. In fact, most everything could have been different. Understanding why it happened as it did, and not some other way, is at the core of historical inquiry.

Unfortunately much of history tends to be written in a manner that depicts the actual outcome as inevitable. Incredibly close elections (think John F. Kennedy's election in 1960) are depicted as if they were the inevitable result of certain trends in American life. Important stories such as the triumph of the "Patriots" over the "Loyalists" in our war for independence from Great Britain, the outcome of the Civil War, American involvement in World War II, and the Cuban Missile Crisis are often described as if circumstances and individuals came together to execute a result preordained by some unknown shaper of human destiny. Even though at some level we know this is clearly not so, our minds tend to absorb it that way.

Of course understanding why things came out the way they did is complex. It takes hard work, digging through original materials, open-minded analysis, and the willingness to reconsider. Partly through close examination of many taped conversations of the Executive Committee of the National Security Council, historian Sheldon Stern has argued persuasively in *The Cuban Missile Crisis in American Memory: Myths versus Reality* that almost everything most people think they know about the Cuban Missile Crisis is mistaken. This is especially true about the events leading up to the crisis, which most see as having arisen nearly out of the blue due to provocative acts taken by dangerously unstable Soviet leaders. In fact, having argued in the 1960 election that there was a significant missile gap and that America was at an increasing disadvantage in the arms race, our newly elected president, John Kennedy, and his unpredictable and aggressive brother, Attorney General Robert Kennedy, were hell-bent on being seen as hawkish guardians of American security. Immediately after he took office, consistent with his campaign rhetoric, JFK approved placing Jupiter missiles in Turkey and Italy, significantly increasing our ability to hit Soviet targets in a first strike. With that in mind, Khrushchev's decision to place Soviet missiles in Cuba was not in fact an out-of-the-blue unilateral act of aggression, but more a clumsy, blustery response to the Jupiter missiles and other American actions. Stern's analysis of the taped deliberations within the administration reveals that our elected and military leaders understood this context. But you would not learn this from most history textbooks and certainly not from popular movies, and it is not the story held in our collective "American Memory."

And what about World War II? With hindsight, the grotesque, over-the-top, almost cartoonish militarism of Japanese imperialism and the even more evil-demon, ghoulish horror show of their Nazi allies appear doomed for defeat in a world supposedly moving in some "arc" toward justice. But clearly it could have been otherwise, at least for a long period of time.

It was possible, if not probable, that America could have remained on the sidelines long enough for the Germans and Japanese to consolidate their gains and remake the map of world power. What forces convinced a massively reluctant American public that aiding the allies, preparing for war, and then entering it after the Japanese strike on Pearl Harbor—on two fronts—was both necessary and right?

Philip Roth has given us a fictional alternative reality to America's entry into the war in his novel *The Plot Against America*. Written from the point of view of Philip Roth at seven years old, *The Plot Against America* tells what happens when isolationist hero Charles Lindbergh is nominated by the Republican Party and defeats FDR in the 1940 presidential election. The novel captures the potential for America to succumb to its darker side, sliding slowly into fascism and institutional anti-Semitism. These were among the undercurrents of the influential "America First" isolationist movement led by such disparate figures as Kingman Brewster, Sinclair Lewis, and Henry Ford, and whose student chapters included John F. Kennedy.

The novel opens: "Fear presides over these memories, a perpetual fear. Of course no childhood is without its terrors, yet I wonder if I would have been a less frightened boy if Lindbergh hadn't been president or if I hadn't been the offspring of Jews."

Lindbergh is the central figure of the novel and was a major figure in American life following his heroic 1927 flight across the Atlantic in the *Spirit of Saint Louis* and the tragic death of his son at the hands of a kidnapper five years later. And although he did exert enormous influence, he was "unrealized" in the sense that his potential influence and power were even greater.

Like Joseph Kennedy, Lindbergh saw the British as the past and the Germans as the future. His faulty moral compass did not register that a Nazi future might be organizationally efficient but horrific in ways that matter a great deal more. While not a Nazi himself, he was susceptible to the flattery of Nazi officials, and, as an airman, he was impressed by the dominance of the German air force. He was committed to strict neutrality and worked with the many American military officials opposed to FDR's plans to aid the British war effort and initiate a peace-time draft. The charming, handsome, and aloof Lindbergh was both naïve and unschooled in the ways of politics. Yet, as the 1940 election loomed, had he been a candidate, he would have made a far more likely Republican nominee than the one who actually emerged, Wendell Willkie, and perhaps a far more likely winner.

As recounted in Lynne Olson's new book *Those Angry Days: Roosevelt, Lindbergh, and America's Fight Over World War II, 1939–1941*, Willkie's candidacy is one of those unlikely yet influential events that tipped the scales of history. In 1940 FDR was popular but unsteady following the defeat of his plan to "pack" the Supreme Court with New Deal supporters, and he was especially wary of taking steps

WENDELL WILLKIE
Harris & Ewing

toward war preparation that might endanger his re-election. No other president had ever sought a third term and with that "power grab" as a background, he knew that his many enemies might galvanize the electorate around an agenda of "peace above all else."

Willkie won the Republican nomination over the far better known Robert Taft, Thomas Dewey, and Arthur Vandenberg. He was certainly an unlikely candidate to lead a Republican Party that had grown increasingly conservative and isolationist, for he was neither. A former Democrat, he is the only major party candidate for president who never held major elected or appointed public office or high military rank. He had spent his career as a lawyer and a businessman and had supported many New Deal programs while opposing others as anti-business. He began the campaign as more of an internationalist than FDR, claiming, in fact, that FDR had not been aggressive enough in preparing the nation for war.

It is true that at times during the campaign Willkie faltered in his disposition not to demagogue the issue of war preparation. But considering the alternatives, explored in *The Plot Against America* and *Those Angry Days*, the Willkie campaign is an example of how politicians can run campaigns within certain boundaries in times when such boundaries are badly needed.

A week after the election, Willkie said, "We have elected Franklin Roosevelt president. He is your president. He is my president." And he spent the next four years (sadly his last, as he died in 1944) working with FDR. He supported the 1941 Lend-Lease bill sending military equipment to the British and traveled abroad as FDR's personal representative to Britain, China, and the Soviet Union. He spoke out for civil rights for African Americans and worked with Eleanor Roosevelt to found Freedom House.

In a December 1, 2012 *New York Times* article headlined "When Partisans Became Partners," Williams College historian Susan Dunn wrote of the Roosevelt-Willkie partnership. She ends the piece recounting a story about FDR overhearing his aide Harry Hopkins disparaging Willkie. FDR snapped, saying, "Don't ever say anything like that around here again. Don't even think it. You of all people ought to know that we might not have had Lend-Lease or Selective Service or a lot of other things if it hadn't been for Wendell Willkie. He was a godsend to this country when we needed him most."

But we know it did not need to be that way. Histories such as Olson's and Dunn's, as well as Roth's novel, show how close we came to a much darker journey. Wendell Willkie is part of an unlikely story. And although he died having been repudiated and humiliated by the Republican Party, he deserves our respectful attention today for displaying qualities sorely lacking in most of our present-day "leaders."

Dunn suggests that Willkie was at peace with his choices. He told a friend, "If I could write my own epitaph and if I had to choose between saying, 'Here lies an unimportant president' or 'Here lies one who contributed to saving freedom at a moment of great peril,' I would prefer the latter."

April 2013

THE BEST PRESIDENT OF OUR LIFETIME?

A TOPIC OF conversation at a few recent dinner parties has been picking the best president of our lifetimes. The guests have mostly been in their fifties or sixties and have chosen to limit the debate to the presidents who have served since 1952, thus excluding FDR and Truman. The guests evidence a pronounced progressive bent. When pushed to pick, most struggle with their choice. Of the thirty or so ballots cast at these dinners, the president with the most votes is Lyndon Johnson, although everyone who votes for him feels obliged to explain how they could possibly overlook his escalation of the war in Vietnam. Very few dinner guests voted for the president ranked highest in this group by most historians—Dwight Eisenhower, a Republican.

I was born in the Eisenhower years but have always had a rather murky sense of his political and military leadership. Over this past holiday I read Jean Edward Smith's biography, *Eisenhower in War and Peace*.

I enjoyed the book, but finished it with less insight into Eisenhower than I expected after 766 pages. Smith seems to anticipate that Eisenhower's elusive qualities might leave the reader feeling a bit empty. He closes his book with the story of how David Eisenhower asked his grandmother, Mamie, whether she felt she had really known Dwight David Eisenhower. "I'm not sure anyone did," Mamie replied.

The book made me nostalgic for the times when there were middle-of-the-road Republicans. It also made me ponder the costs to the country of the Republican Party's conversion to what is often mistakenly called "conservatism," but which is more accurately described as "extremist" or "radical."

Eisenhower was not ideological. If you had to describe him in such terms you might call him a progressive conservative, a label with which I imagine he would be comfortable.

Coming to power just a few years after the New Deal, he had no desire to roll back any of FDR's reforms. In most ways he was remarkably non-political. Not one of his original cabinet appointees was a professional politician.

As president he often got more support from Democrats than Republicans in Congress, and although he was slow to speak out against them, he detested Joseph McCarthy and his ilk. He opposed multiple efforts by the military and others to get the United States into a war during his presidency, although he did support several misguided covert actions. He is the only president of the twentieth century to preside over eight years of peace and prosperity.

Perhaps Eisenhower's three most important legacies are the interstate highway system, one of the largest public works projects in U.S. history; his five Supreme Court appointments, including four justices who played crucial roles on the interventionist Warren Court—Earl Warren, Potter Stewart, John Marshall Harlan, and William Brennan; and the "farewell address" that he gave at the end of his presidency. That speech, which he worked on for over a month, warned of the dangers to the country from what he called the emerging "military industrial complex."

Due to Cold War tensions, he said that "we have been compelled to create a permanent armaments industry of vast proportions…three-and-a-half million men and women are directly engaged in the defense establishment. We annually spend more on military security than the net income of all United States corporations."

He pointed out that this was new to the American experience and warned that "we must guard against the acquisition of unwarranted influence…by the military industrial complex. The potential for the disastrous rise of misplaced power exists and will persist."

Eisenhower called his moderate politics "Modern Republicanism." Later it came to be called Rockefeller Republicanism after New York governor and presidential hopeful Nelson Rockefeller.

It is difficult to remember now that there was a vibrant liberal and moderate wing of the Republican Party well into the early 1980s. Progressive Republicans were especially prominent in the U.S. Senate where George Aiken of Vermont, Clifford Case of New Jersey, Jacob Javits of New York, Mark Hatfield of Oregon, Charles Percy of Illinois, Charles Mathias of Maryland, and Edward Brooke of Massachusetts (the first popularly elected African American senator) spoke up for civil rights and anti-poverty programs and against the war in Vietnam. Proportionally more Republicans voted for the 1964 Civil Rights Act than Democrats.

There is an important story to be told here. (I have not read it yet but reviewers say that Geoffrey Kabaservice tells this story well in his recent *Rule and Ruin: The Downfall of Moderation and the Destruction of the Republican Party, From Eisenhower to the Tea Party*.)

When Eisenhower left the White House in 1961, he was as popular as when he entered it eight years earlier. It is unlikely that anyone that day foresaw that fifty years later, almost all "Eisenhower Republicans" would have been run out of the Republican Party.

To those of us living in the new dynamic, one thing is apparent: the loss of such figures dramatically reduces the problem-solving capacity of American democracy.

For democratic politics to work there need to be leaders willing to put "getting critical tasks accomplished" above both partisanship and ideology. Such leaders are in short supply today, and, consequentially, we are unable to grapple with our most pressing problems.

It is worth remembering that it was not always that way. Eisenhower may not appeal much to those of us desirous of dramatic calls to action. But his quiet, stable, seasoned leadership and willingness to strive for consensus on what might move us forward arguably make him the most successful president of the last half century.

January 2014

THE ROOSEVELTS

I INTRODUCED Ken Burns' documentary, *The Roosevelts: An Intimate History,* at two preview showings at the Little Art Theater here in Yellow Springs. I have seldom accepted speaking engagements about "being a Roosevelt" as I am not comfortable with public conversations about the matter. But that does not mean I have not wrestled with this legacy as well as the extraordinary multi-faceted privilege it has brought.

This privilege is partly about money, although over the years the money dissipated due to heavy spending and government-scale salaries. Even TR scrambled for money, writing for *Scribner's Magazine* to pay for his overseas adventures. And, as I learned from a recent book, my parents borrowed money from my governess. But the point is—I had a governess. And when I had open heart surgery as a child, my parents may have borrowed the money to pay for it, but the surgeon who performed the operation was the best in the country.

This privilege is also about access to great schools and beautiful places and people willing to let me in their homes, offices, or hearts because of what my relatives did and what they meant to them.

And that is perhaps the most exceptional part of this privilege: being well-thought of without having done anything to earn it, and well-thought of by people that…well…that you would want to be well-thought of by.

As it tends to eclipse or at least diminish my own need to be well-thought of on my own, I have run from this.

My office is festooned with pictures of a great president I have studied at enormous length and revere—Abraham Lincoln.

When I sought to go into politics I stayed away from New York, where my family has been in public service for well over a century.

I avoid Roosevelt family reunions.

And yet—I have studied TR, ER, and FDR at great length, greatly admire and love them, am proud to be in some relationship with their political legacy, and watched this series with rapt attention and seldom with dry eyes.

I inherited much from them, including a complex relationship with privilege. Another inheritance is that I believe great deference should be given to the person doing the work. I would hand the excerpt below from TR's "It is not the critic who counts" speech to countless individuals had it not been given by my great-grandfather:

It is not the critic who counts; not the man who points out how the strong man stumbles, or where the doer of deeds could have done them better. The credit belongs to the man who is actually in the arena, whose face is marred by dust and sweat and blood; who strives valiantly; who errs, who comes short again and again, because there is no effort without error and shortcoming; but who does actually strive to do the deeds; who knows great enthusiasms, the great devotions; who spends himself in a worthy cause; who at the best knows in

ELEANOR ROOSEVELT
Library of Congress

the end the triumph of high achievement, and who at the worst, if he fails, at least fails while daring greatly, so that his place shall never be with those cold and timid souls who neither know victory nor defeat.

I love that—"those cold and timid souls who neither know victory nor defeat."

"Noblesse Oblige" is complicated.

I leaf through my father's 1936 Groton School yearbook and then my own from 1974 at Saint Albans School. Mine has African American and Jewish faces and a good deal of scruffiness. His has all white faces with recognizable last names all—literally all—headed to Harvard, Yale, or Princeton. And yet they are more similar than different and, of course, both are suffused with privilege.

I ponder the influence of two Episcopalian headmasters of these schools who preached duty, obligation, hard work, and sacrifice.

I ponder the effects of significant illness on a person, especially the effects of childhood illness.

I ponder my fear of being perceived in certain ways and my often overabundant anger at relatives who have coasted through their lives and at Bill Weld, the self-satisfied patrician Republican, once married to my cousin, against whom I ran for governor of Massachusetts.

I think about complex relations with a father's legacy. TR worshipped his father but was humiliated that he bought his way out of fighting in the Civil War. My own father was a CIA agent. His inscription to me of his book about the 1953 American intervention in Iran—*Countercoup*—was signed "from your reprehensible father." When younger that was the source of unattractive pride to me—now it just makes me very sad.

And I ponder again the meaning of privilege and its connection with tragedy. TR lost his wife and mother on the same day. ER was orphaned at nine. FDR contracted polio in his thirties, never walked again, endured enormous pain and humiliation, and hid his disability from the nation he served. Without these tragedies they would not have been the people they became. In this documentary we witness these privileged people transformed by adversity and observe how this adversity catalyzed incredible resolve and cemented a sense of purpose that rose far above mere political ambition.

Of course their historical legacy is profound. I highlight four interconnected aspects to this legacy:

1. The historian Gordon Woods notes how highly the Founders valued "disinterestedness," a quality lost to most now but distinctly different from uninterested or indifferent.

    Samuel Johnson defined disinterest as "superior to regard of private advantage; not influenced by private profit." It means even more than that to me. It means the ability to rise above self-interest or even the advantage of the moment to see things as fairly as possible and to do what is best regardless of the obstacles.

    I believe that, in the main, is what TR, ER, and FDR did.

2. They had a deep abiding belief in the obligations of government and were committed to "The Public Good."
3. They never bought into the theory of market supremacy or of any monopoly of virtue held by those who had "made it." Quite the contrary, they knew what privilege brought and the role that luck plays in life.
4. Because of the above, they dramatically expanded the role of the presidency and the federal government in the lives of Americans.

The documentary makes clear how connected they were. TR was a personal inspiration for Eleanor, his favorite niece, and also for FDR. And his Square Deal was the platform on which the New Deal was built.

TR saw moneyed interests as guilty of "all forms of iniquity from the oppression of wage workers to defrauding the public." FDR inherited this derisive attitude to "the malefactors of great wealth." Ponder for a moment FDR's speech at Madison Square Garden four days before his 1936 re-election.

> *Tonight I call the roll—the roll of honor of those who stood with us in 1932 and still stand with us today.*
>
> *Written on it are the names of millions who never had a chance—men at starvation wages, women in sweatshops, children at looms…*
>
> *For twelve years this Nation was afflicted with hear-nothing, see-nothing, do-nothing Government. The Nation looked to Government but the Government looked away…*

> *Powerful influences strive today to restore that kind of government with its doctrine that that Government is best which is most indifferent.*
>
> *For nearly four years you have had an Administration which instead of twirling its thumbs has rolled up its sleeves. We will keep our sleeves rolled up.*
>
> *We had to struggle with the old enemies—business and financial monopoly, speculation, reckless banking, class antagonism.*
>
> *They had begun to consider the Government of the United States as a mere appendage to their own affairs…*
>
> *Never before in all our history have these forces been so united against one candidate as they stand today. They are unanimous in their hate for me—and I welcome their hatred.*
>
> *I should like to have it said of my first Administration that in it the forces of selfishness and of lust for power met their match. I should like to have it said of my second Administration that in it these forces met their master.*

Can you imagine any elected official in America today saying anything remotely like this?

They had a very firm sense of their own rightness, although of course they were not always right. TR was a bellicose imperialist fond of war and killing. FDR approved the internment of Japanese American citizens during World War II. Despite some significant strides, they both moved too slowly on racial issues.

All three are described as "traitors to their class." But it is much more complex than that. They are products of their privilege as much as they are antagonists to it. Their beliefs and actions fall into the now lost world where many believed government must rise above the fray, especially class interest, and administer justice—to be "disinterested."

All politicians have a need to be loved and the three Roosevelts were no exception. But they were also not afraid to be hated by those who sought to shape government to their own personal agenda and away from "the public good." Decency and the courage to fight when fighting is called for is not a class phenomenon. It is a personal one.

The series delves deep and has a sweet lyrical bent. It caused me to reflect on the timid, sadly diminished politics of our time. It reignited the guilt I have felt that I did not stay in politics and keep fighting—that in that arena at least, I lacked my ancestors' grit and resolve.

I hugely admire their extraordinary courage and am grateful for what they accomplished and what they meant to this country. And I, hopefully among many others, know—*really know*—how desperately we need such voices to be heard again.

September 2014

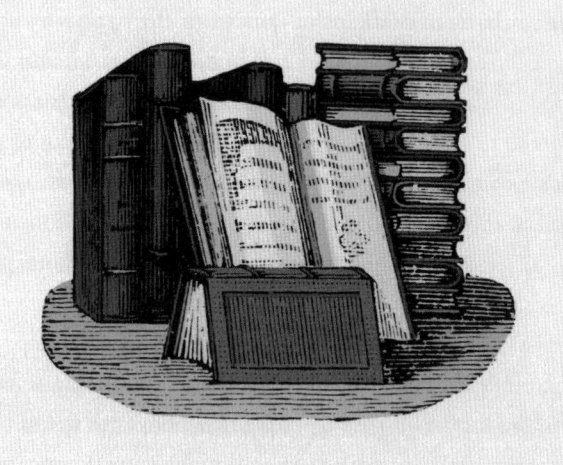

CURRENT EVENTS

THE RISE OF WOMEN, INEQUALITY, AND OUR TIMID POLITICS

THE APRIL 13, 2012 *New York Times Sunday Book Review* contains an article on Liza Mundy's new book, *The Richer Sex: How the New Majority of Female Breadwinners is Transforming Sex, Love, and Family*. This is becoming, finally, big news. On March 26, 2012, the book was *Time* magazine's cover story.

What is going on? A great deal, and probably much more than we yet know. We do know that for quite a while now male wages have been stagnant while female wages keep rising. We know that women in dual-earner families now earn 47 percent of family earnings, that approximately 40 percent of employed wives outearn their husbands, and that young single women outearn their male counterparts in every major American city. And we know that these trends are accelerating fast. Education is an area of particularly dramatic change. Women now earn 57 percent of all bachelor degrees and comprise 60 percent of all graduate students. At small liberal arts schools such as Antioch, women outnumber men by numbers that increase every year. Seventy percent of our accepted students this year are women. And perhaps most significantly, even before the ramifications of this shift in educational achievement are fully felt in the marketplace, women already hold more than half,

51 percent, of the most prestigious job classifications—jobs deemed to be "management and professional."

It is also important to remember that a stubbornly resistant wage gap remains, even if it may not last much longer and is much smaller for younger women. More importantly, there are significant "lagging indicators." For example, as Meg Wolitzer noted in "The Second Shelf" (*New York Times Book Review*, March 30, 2012), "women who write literary fiction frequently find themselves in an unjust world," struggling to make it to "the upper shelf." And men still dominate critical places of power—in politics, high-level judicial positions, and corporate leadership. These will likely be even more resistant to change than the overall wage gap, as they represent deep cultural identifications that will likely outlast trends bubbling up from beneath.

But the bubbling is profound and the questions raised are equally so. Mundy asks, "In what way, if at all, do the sexes need each other now that the old economic bonds have been broken?" That is a very long way from being worked out, and Mundy's take on it—that these changes will be freeing to both men and women—is far more optimistic than many others. Men are floundering. Men continue to rate forging deep personal relationships less important than women do, and in April the Pew Research Center reported that men are now also less ambitious in the workplace. Sixty-six percent of women ages eighteen to thirty-four rated career high on their list of priorities, compared with only fifty-nine percent of young men. So what, one might wonder, is the focus of young men today?

Of course it is also good for us at Antioch to ask what we should learn from this data. Because of our full-tuition Horace Mann Fellowship as well as other factors, the students coming to Antioch tend to be from families at the lower end of the economic ladder. And the status of boys and men is declining faster in this stratum than in more privileged ones. Young men who are not from privilege get into college in lower numbers and drop out of college in much higher numbers. Overall, American colleges do not offer sufficient supports for struggling students, and Antioch's retention rates in the past have not always been strong. We must be prepared to offer multiple academic and non-academic supports to all our students, but will need a particular strategy for young men.

Meanwhile, perhaps the most alarming of all recent trends—the dramatic growth in wealth and income inequality—has reached a level only seen right before the Great Depression. But again, most people seem only dimly aware of how astounding and unusual this trend is in historical terms. The April 16, 2012 *New York Times* contains an article, "For Two Economists, the Buffett Rule Is Just a Start," about the Frenchmen Emmanuel Saez, who teaches at Berkeley, and Thomas Piketty, who teaches at the Paris School of Economics. They offer a little history lesson, and have a twist, with which I sympathize, on the word "radical." In remarking on how the proposed Buffett Rule, a thirty percent minimum tax on incomes over $1 million, would do very little to reverse the extensive gains of the top one percent in recent decades, Piketty says "that the United States is getting accustomed to a completely crazy level of inequality. People say that reducing inequality is radical. I think that tolerating the level of inequality the United States tolerates is radical."

And they point out that it does not need to be this way, nor, unlike what many people think, has it always been this way. "In a way, the Unites States is becoming like Old Europe, which is very strange in historical perspective," Piketty says in the article. "The United States used to be very egalitarian, not just in words but in actuality. Inequality of wealth and income used to be much larger in France. And very high taxes on the rich—that was invented in the United States." Since incomes of the top one percent grew an astounding ninety-four percent from 2000 to 2007 alone, proposals such as the Buffett thirty percent rate are actually very modest relative to historical norms. Despite this fact, they get described as "radical" attempts at "massive wealth redistribution." What is actually aberrational are the current tax rates, as the marginal rates on high incomes are near historic lows. That rate was ninety-one percent while FDR was president and stayed above fifty percent until Reagan's presidency.

Ah, history. Historians should note how much the political dialogue and rhetoric has changed, and that today's rhetoric obscures the radical income gains of the very wealthy, the truth about our historically low tax rates on upper-income earners, and the extraordinarily limited political debate about what tax policies make sense at this time. Instead, the media seriously report charges of "socialism" and "class warfare" leveled at President Obama, whose policies, like those of former President Clinton, are those of a moderate to conservative Democrat. Let us remember that in 2010, President Obama, supported by Clinton, acquiesced to Republican demands to extend the regressive Bush tax cuts—despite the fact that these tax advantages go primarily to upper-income Americans. That same year we began the soft recovery from a very harsh recession, and ninety-three percent of the resulting economic gains went to the top one percent.

To give much-needed perspective to this debate, journalists should report on earlier fights in the twentieth century, when, unlike today, rhetorical vitriol went both ways. One telling example would be to look back to FDR at the end of his bitter 1936 campaign for re-election. At a rally at Madison Square Garden, surrounded on the stage by his patrician family, he spoke about the rich and powerful in ways unimaginable from a prominent elected official today.

"They had begun to consider the government of the United States as a mere appendage of their own affairs. We know that government by organized money is as dangerous as government by organized mob. Never before in history have these forces been so united against one candidate as they stand today. They are unanimous in their hate for me, and I welcome their hatred."

Now, that sounds a bit like "class warfare." And this reminder of past debates should open up a useful discussion of why the political response to the Great Depression was so much more robust than the response to our recent economic crisis. Along those lines, the *Times* article ends with Piketty observing that the Buffett Rule's proposed thirty percent tax rate "is three times smaller than the 91% of Roosevelt. And inequality is greater than in the time of Roosevelt."

But listening to most of the political dialogue today, who would know it?

Colleges have a responsibility to lend perspective to the debates of the day. These perspectives must not be dictated by adherence to a particular political philosophy; in fact, we serve our students poorly if they are asked to wrestle with limited ideologies. Students should understand the anger of both Tea Party and Occupy activists, and they should understand their historical roots. And they should begin to contemplate, as should we all, how these profound changes in American economic and cultural life will shape our country in the years ahead.

April 2012

SOME GOOD NEWS AND WORRIES ABOUT HIGHER EDUCATION

THIS MONTH I make note of three facts or trends that may surprise you and comment on *Paying for the Party: How College Maintains Inequality*, a book that casts doubt on both the effectiveness and the fairness of much of American higher education.

It is remarkable to me how significant demographic shifts get so little attention. I have written before about the changing status of women in higher education and the workforce, the decline of marriage and of children being brought up by two parents, and the rapid increase in people living alone. This month I remark on three underreported changes that have received a bit of attention in the past few weeks, but are far more significant in their implications than has been observed.

I am happy to report that all three of these trends are hopeful indicators.

I need hopeful signs. The mounting evidence of decline and erosion in both current living standards and future prospects makes it a challenge for me to maintain my self-image as a "cheerful pessimist." It is the "cheerful" that I worry about losing, as I believe that we are in an age of dizzying change, much of it driven by technological innovations of dubious value, which gives the appearance rather than the substance of progress.

So, here's some good news.

Under-reported fact #1—Amidst all the challenges of improving K–12 education, 2010 data confirms the now decade-long upward movement in the nation's overall high school graduation rate, which is now seventy-eight percent.* Although we have just gotten back to the rates we saw in the early seventies, this still represents significant progress. If we could develop a comprehensive workforce preparation strategy so non-college-bound high school graduates (as well as dropouts) get the additional skill training they need for the new economy, we might well make considerable gains in combating inequality and poverty.

Under-reported fact #2—This past year Hispanic high school graduates surpassed whites in the rate of college enrollment. Sixty-nine percent of Hispanic high school graduates enrolled in college, while sixty-seven percent of white high school graduates enrolled. In the last decade Hispanic high school dropout rates improved much faster than the overall rate. It is also reported that Hispanic families increasingly view college as critical to a better life, and do so more than other demographic groups. This data portends significant changes in the American economic and cultural landscape.

Under-reported fact #3—In 2012, for the first time in history, the percentage of African Americans voting in an election exceeded that of the white population. For those of us involved in progressive politics over a long period of time, the differing turnout percentages of racial and economic groups have been a worry for decades. Poor people and people of color have historically voted in much lower percentages.

---

* As of February 2015, it had risen to 81%.

We know that in many previous elections, including some where the final tally was not even that close, the results would have been different had all segments of the population voted in the same percentages. If 2012's numbers are a reliable future indicator, and not simply a reflection of support for Barack Obama, it points to major changes ahead in the electoral landscape.

Now you will have to hang on to the good feelings this data induces as you examine other pronounced trends in higher education, namely poor graduation rates, dubious learning outcomes for many of those who do graduate, and questionable fairness in the application of scholarship dollars increasingly granted on the basis of "merit" rather than need.

I spent a great deal of my working life in K–12 education, a sector under intense scrutiny since *A Nation at Risk* was published in 1983, and have observed the uncomfortable responses scrutiny usually induces—defensiveness and stubborn resistance are as common as they are unproductive. You hear these responses from many in higher education today as they circle the wagons rather than consider sensible alternatives to current practices.

Of course the causes of many of higher education's problems are complex, as is made clear in *Paying for the Party: How College Maintains Inequality*. Written by Elizabeth Armstrong and Laura Hamilton, sociologists from the University of Michigan at Ann Arbor and the University of California at Merced, respectively, *Paying for the Party* focuses on life at a flagship midwestern state university and adds depth to many of the conclusions of 2011's *Academically Adrift: Limited Learning on College Campuses*. That study, by Richard Arum and Josipa Roksa, reports that as many as thirty-six percent of all college students learn almost nothing in their four years of schooling and highlights large state schools as places where it is easy to do very little work and absorb very little knowledge, yet still graduate with a "marketable" grade point average.

Paying for the Party describes the culture that is contributing to that lack of learning and how we got there. Armstrong and Hamilton demonstrate how declining government support for public higher education contributes to state schools' focus on recruiting out-of-state students with the ability to pay higher tuitions. To attract these students, colleges devote substantial resources to the social and athletic components of college life. The authors note how prevalent the "party pathway" has become and how it serves the economic and social interests, if not the educational needs, of the already advantaged at the expense of those more on the "outside," for whom college is an economic and social challenge of a very different kind. *Paying for the Party* helps us understand the destructive nature of the "arms race" as colleges build increasingly luxurious dormitories and invest in other amenities, such as opulent new athletic centers, in order to win the contest for the shrinking pool of available students from families with the dollars to pay full or near-full tuition.

Think about the messages we are sending. The emphasis on physical plant amenities and athletics, as well as the spending, likely contributes to the culture that allows for lax study habits and low academic ambitions documented in *Academically Adrift* and bemoaned by many who teach these unengaged and unmotivated students.

Causation is a complicated matter. But if we do indeed reap what we sow, the fact that many students view college as essentially a four-year paid vacation is tied to decisions about who colleges seek to serve. Colleges, of course, say they have no choice—that in this era of greatly reduced government support, they must recruit those who can pay, and offer them the amenities and campus culture that will draw them to their schools.

I doubt that we actually intend to accelerate our national decline by reducing academic standards and access to education for the less fortunate, but that is what is happening. Even the statistic cited earlier about growing college-going rates among Hispanic youth is blunted by examining how few of these primarily first-generation students are attending rigorous four-year schools.

Don't underestimate the effects of all of this. Our social and economic mobility rates used to be among the best of the wealthier nations; they now rank near the bottom. In researching his book on American inequality, *The Great Divergence*, Timothy Noah discovered that mobility is now so uncommon that today "parentage is a greater determinant of a man's future earnings than it is of his height and weight." Higher education needs to examine what it is doing to contribute to this, and those of us privileged to work at values-driven institutions such as Antioch need to tackle this issue head on, every day, in all that we do and say. *May 2013*

THE COST OF GROWTH—*THE SIXTH EXTINCTION* AND *THE END OF THE WILD*

FOR THE LAST few months, I have avoided writing about species extinction, the loss of the wild, and how human encroachment is changing all facets of life on Earth. I find it difficult to write about because it is so painful. And I knew that if I wrote about it, there could be no sugarcoating or half-heartedness. I would have to face it—squarely. And, most days, the subject seems too much to take on, too much to absorb.

Of course, I am not alone in my avoidance. Our governmental bodies, mainstream media, and almost all of our brethren not employed by environmental organizations are deep in denial about what is happening and what it will likely mean.

Large issues, including the most important issues we face—even arguably the most important issues that we have ever faced—get pushed aside in favor of the daily drama of human life. While amazing, I suppose it is not surprising. A vast majority of people struggle with just getting by and making do. And no matter our economic circumstances, each of us struggles with the often overwhelming emotional and psychological demands of our existence: our grasping, clumsy attempts to make some sense of our lives and come to terms with the chaos, uncertainty, and cruelty of our world.

Rich or poor, most of us spend our lives pursuing the comforts that industrialism and consumer capitalism afford us. And the man-made world that our constant desire for more is creating is transforming everything else on the planet. All forms of life and all planetary and atmospheric ecosystems, including the climate, are being forced to adapt to rapidly expanding human influence and encroachment. Plant and animal species are going extinct at unparalleled rates and, as a result, the diversity of life is rapidly diminishing. Most species exit quietly but some "systems" strike back; the atmosphere is responding violently—with consequences we can perhaps only begin to imagine—to the man-made emissions that are changing its component parts.

We are changing our world faster and more comprehensively than we had ever thought possible.

We may not have known what we were doing. As Philip Larkin wrote in "Going, Going," his beautiful elegiac poem about the loss of rural England, "most things are never meant." But we now have fair warning about the consequences of our heedless growth. Yet those warnings are getting scant attention and thus far our reaction is stunningly passive.

There is not even much talk, no less action. The most powerful engine of our encroachment—human population growth—was discussed more often in the sixties and seventies than it is today. In those decades people were alarmed that the population had doubled, from two to four billion, in only a half century. (Paul Ehrlich's *The Population Bomb* was published in 1968.) It is doubling again; we add 200,000 people every day, 70 million people every year, and will reach 8 billion people by 2030.

Much of what is written about these matters, while persuasive, somehow lacks the necessary drama. That is how I felt about Elizabeth Kolbert's detailed and well-documented *The Sixth Extinction: An Unnatural History*.

This should be gripping. Stephen Meyer's short, depressing account of what is transpiring, *The End of the Wild*, opens with a heart-stopping, precise summary of where we stand today:

> *For the past several billion years evolution on Earth has been driven by small-scale incremental forces, such as sexual selection, punctuated by cosmic-scale disruptions—plate tectonics, planetary geo-chemistry, global climate shifts, and even extraterrestrial asteroids. Sometime in the last century that changed. Today the guiding hand of natural selection is unmistakably human, with potentially Earth-shaking consequences.*
>
> *The fossil record and contemporary field studies suggest that the average rate of extinction over the past hundred million years has hovered at several species per year. Today the extinction rate surpasses 3,000 species per year and is accelerating rapidly; it may soon reach the tens of thousands. In contrast, new species are appearing at a rate of less than one per year.*
>
> *Over the next 100 years or so as many as a half of the Earth's species, representing a quarter of the planet's genetic stock, will functionally if not completely disappear. The land and the oceans will continue to teem with life, but it will be a peculiarly homogenized*

assemblage of organisms unnaturally selected for their compatibility with one fundamental force: us. Nothing—not national or international laws, global bio-reserves, local sustainability schemes, or even "wild lands" fantasies—can change the current course. The broad path for biological evolution is now set for the next several million years. And in this sense the extinction crisis—the race to save the composition, structure, and organization of biodiversity as it exists today—is over, and we have lost.

What could be more dramatic? Man has spent centuries subduing nature, believing, somehow, that we were a species apart, above it all due to our capacity to reason. Yet our heedless destruction of our own nest prompts comparisons with other species we tend to find humorous or pathetic—ostriches with their heads in the sand or perhaps better yet lemmings, who supposedly engage in large-scale species suicide.

And our heedless growth and lack of concern for its long-term effects does take on the appearance of suicide. If Meyer and others are right that we have indeed "lost" the battle to maintain biodiversity and control climate change and are now headed toward an uncertain but likely dark future, we have done all of this without even putting up a fight, or applying our capacity to "reason." There have been no real global alarms or concerted international action. There has certainly been no leadership coming from our own country, the largest consumer of goods of all sorts, including fossil fuels.

Just one day's newspaper provides evidence of the odd dichotomy between the mounting evidence of dramatic changes in our ecosystem caused by human activity and our inability to make even small changes in our behavior. Take Tuesday, May 13, 2014, for example. That day the front page of the *New York Times* featured a story on scientists warning about polar melt, predicting that melting will ultimately result in a ten-foot rise in sea levels. The article quotes Thomas Wager from NASA saying that this "is really happening. There's no stopping it now." Within that paper's front section is another story reporting that the hyper-partisan U.S. Senate was unable to take action on a modest energy efficiency bill with many small-step provisions to cut energy use and create new incentives for more energy-efficient heating and cooling systems.

Within the environmental movement there is a debate about the appropriate level of despair versus a perceived political need to offer hope. On April 19, 2014, the *New York Times Magazine* profiled the British environmental activist Paul Kingsnorth, founder of the Dark Mountain Project, which is dedicated to helping people come to terms with the "the age of ecocide." Having spent years in the environmental movement trying to catalyze change, Kingsnorth has given up. He believes it is dishonest to offer hope when there is none. In 2012 he told an interviewer, "whenever I hear the word 'hope' these days, I reach for my whiskey bottle." He even wonders whether he wants civilization as it exists today to prevail.

Kingsnorth's new position has drawn a great deal of criticism from activists still "in the game." They argue that although some negative events are now beyond our control, the extent of the damage is still to be determined. As Elizabeth Kolbert stated in the April 14, 2014 *New Yorker,* "The fact that so much time has been wasted standing around means that the problem of climate change is now much more difficult to deal with than it was when it was first identified. But this only makes the imperative to act that much greater, because, as one set of grim predictions is being borne out, another, even worse set remains to be written."

But if there is serious large-scale thinking about what must be done to change direction, it is almost completely isolated from mainstream culture and politics. Many productive changes are happening at the local level, in places such as Yellow Springs and Antioch, but large-scale actions that might have a chance to turn the tide are glaringly absent.

That may be because the changes that are necessary are so disruptive of our way of living that we are unwilling to contemplate them. We are addicted to our consumer goods and creature comforts, and we are addicted to growth. Our economy depends on it. Our measurements reward it. Liberals and conservatives compete over who can bring more of it.

To envision a world which turns its back on growth, to imagine an alternative measurement is currently beyond our capacity, even though it is readily apparent that this is what the new realities call for. For now at least, it is easier to go on about our business hoping that these myriad warnings are overstated or that somehow technology will provide an easy way out.

Is it any wonder that college students exhibit an odd combination of idealism and lack of hope? It is why few people still look to politics for answers. And why an increasing number of observers and activists such as Kingsnorth conclude that it is time to "come to terms" that we are living in the "age of ecocide."

Alan Weisman's 2007 nonfiction, *The World Without Us*, goes further—starting to envision what the world might be like after humankind destroys itself. But Weisman's book skips a step—the drama and trauma of what it might be like for humankind in the years of our demise. Perhaps that is where we should focus. As the contemplation of such times might, just possibly, be jarring enough to force us into action.

If so, a good place to start is Cormac McCarthy's gruesome post-apocalyptic novel *The Road*. *The Road* begins after the calamity and never explains what it might have been. It follows a father and his son as they attempt to survive in a broken and barren world in which anything that was good—man-made or of the earth—is gone. It is gripping, terrifying, unsentimental, and urgent. The world it depicts is savage, someplace beyond hopeless. People eat people and are thankful that they can. As one reviewer pointed out, the reader "remains unsure whether it is more humane to hope for their survival or hope for their gentle death."

As Janet Maslin concluded in her *New York Times* review: "This is an exquisitely bleak incantation—pure poetic brimstone. Mr. McCarthy has summoned his fiercest visions to invoke the devastation. He gives voice to the unspeakable in a terse cautionary tale that is too potent to be numbing, despite the stupefying ravages it describes. Mr. McCarthy brings an almost biblical fury as he bears witness to sights man was never meant to see...*The Road* offers nothing in the way of escape or comfort. But its fearless wisdom is more indelible than reassurance could ever be."

All the evidence we have is that warnings are not enough. The atmospheric rumblings portending a coming calamity may escalate but by then it will be too late. Reassurance is not what we need. We need words and visions that are "too potent to be numbing." If other creatures on their way out had voice and we had ears to listen, the savage cries of despair of what we have already wrought might indeed be more than we could bear. But what is to come might be much worse.

May 2014

A DEFINING MOMENT, HARDLY NOTICED

RECENTLY, I WAS hit hard by a startling piece of news—as of 2013, *a majority of public school students in the United States come from low-income families*. Significantly, this is a national, not just an urban, problem. For example, low-income students now make up forty percent of our suburban schools.

The immensity of this new reality and its implications is overwhelming.

The percentage of lower-income students has been growing steadily since 1989, when it was thirty-two percent. At that time, folks "in the know" were wringing their hands that one-third of all students were attempting to gain the necessary skills to make it in America while struggling with the myriad demands of living in poverty. I know because I was a legislator in Massachusetts at the time and used this data to advocate for increased state investment in our schools.

Twenty-six years later, the news that we have surpassed the fifty percent mark is being met with mostly…silence.

Ask yourself—have you even seen it reported? *The New York Times* certainly did not see it as big news, placing the story on page 13 of the Saturday, January 17, 2014, paper.

K-12 schools have been dealing with this new reality for some time, and it is important to emphasize that low-income students can be educated to high standards. We know this because organizations such as The Education Trust have been documenting the work of thousands of individual schools that do exactly that. But schools that do this work well offer consistent, high-quality instruction as well as many additional—often expensive—supplementary services. And, since these are not provided by enough of our schools, K-12 has a long way to go to educate the new majority to levels that will allow them to succeed in our increasingly competitive global economy.

But what about higher education? Community colleges and some other schools have made significant changes to accommodate the needs of a new generation of college-goers with entirely different life experiences from their predecessors. But most four-year schools have not yet done so, especially the more prestigious ones, as the large majority of their students come from the top quarter of the American economy. In the greater Dayton area, Wilberforce serves a vast majority of low-income students (over eighty percent), and Wright State's population is well over a third Pell Grant-eligible, but Ohio State University is at twenty-two percent, Miami University is at sixteen percent, and the University of Dayton is at twelve percent.

Most highly ranked liberal arts colleges live in a world that is fading fast. Of all such schools, Vassar, Amherst, and Grinnell serve the highest percentage of Pell Grant-eligible students—about twenty-two percent. Two other liberal arts colleges that are doing groundbreaking work to better serve lower-income students—Bard and Franklin & Marshall—are at nineteen percent and fourteen percent. The other top-ranked schools serve far smaller numbers of what will soon be the new majority of students.

At the re-created Antioch College, these new demographics are already at work—approximately forty-five percent of our students are Pell Grant-eligible. Antioch long ago embraced experiential learning, which research suggests is especially effective for first-generation and low-income students, and we have made additional changes in how we do our work. But we need to make many more. And we have to find new sources of revenue to supplement the loss of tuition dollars.

The academic, cultural, and financial challenges that we are grappling with at Antioch will be faced by many more schools in the years to come.

Despite the meager attention it is receiving, the fact that a majority of children in our public schools are low-income is a defining moment in American life. Wrestling with this new reality is challenging but must be done. It must be talked about, even dwelled on. And certainly not ignored. We have to realize—and accept—that a new day is dawning. Or, more accurately, that a new day *has already dawned*, and it requires more from us and our institutions than we ever could have dreamed.

February 2015

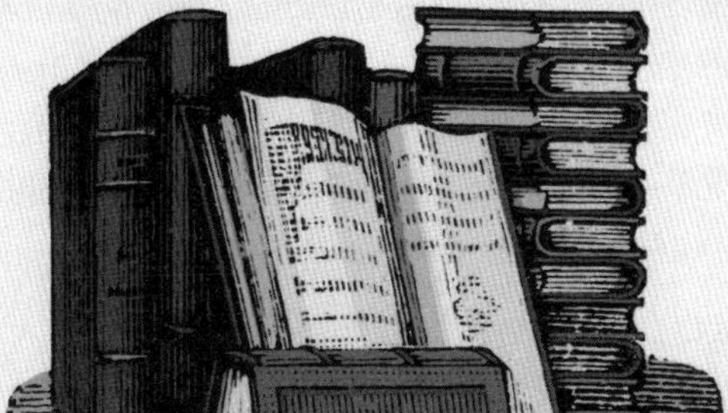

MISCELLANEOUS

RECKONING WITH AMERICA— SURPRISING NEW TELEVISION

MY MOST INTELLECTUALLY charismatic professor in college was Walter Jackson Bate. He taught a course on the Age of Johnson and evidenced a personal connection to Samuel Johnson that had many of us believing that he conversed with the long-deceased philosopher in the middle of the night. He urged us all to spend time with Johnson, to read his essays and Boswell's biography, because "whatever we might be struggling with, wherever we were going, we would meet Johnson on his way back."

Bate's own biography of Johnson is a great book as is his book of literary criticism, *The Burden of the Past and the English Poet*, in which he ponders what happens when the artist asks the question "What is there left to do?" This question arises with special poignancy when you are working immediately after some extraordinary accomplishment has been achieved. In his book, Bate asks, for example, what a playwright does after Shakespeare. From an American perspective we might ask what a composer of popular music should attempt in the aftermath of Berlin, Gershwin, and Rogers & Hammerstein.

Bate argues "that the remorseless deepening of self-consciousness, before the rich and intimidating legacy of the past, has become the greatest single problem that modern art has had to face." He warns of making originality—what Voltaire called "senseless eccentricity" and Bate calls "anti-art"—an objective that trumps others. He clearly saw much of what we call "modern art," whether in classical music, jazz, or the visual arts, fitting into that unhappy pattern. Bate wanted us to see that standing on the shoulders of earlier artists offers the opportunity to see further and more clearly and to consider where opportunities lie to deepen earlier work.

Bate would be happy to see that in America today familiar territory is being richly reimagined across multiple artistic disciplines. For example, this year's well-reviewed western epic, Philipp Meyer's *The Son*, is firmly in the tradition of exploring the West as a way to illuminate the evolution of American character.

The Son is a step in an important transition. The first iteration of western drama depicted white people exercising their "manifest destiny" to gain control of the land from aboriginal savages. Moving on from that limited perspective, novelists such as Larry McMurtry in *Lonesome Dove* saw nobility in all parties. Meyer, too, plays no favorites, but instead of shared nobility he sees a shared inclination to horrific violence that makes modern terrorism look rather mild-mannered. McMurtry's is an affectionate, nostalgic, and sweet-tempered take on the west. His characters are tough but honorable. Mining the same territory, Meyer sees only violence and mayhem.

My old professor would likely be very surprised, as I am, to find that this reworking of how we see ourselves may be manifested most spectacularly on television. Until my wife and I watched HBO's *The Wire*, I glibly dismissed the enthusiastic friends who said we are in the midst of a golden age of extraordinary television. It is difficult to overstate how hard *The Wire* hit us. We watched it in 2008, the year it was cancelled by HBO. We watched all sixty episodes, one after another, transfixed, night after night for perhaps three weeks, until we finished, exhausted, and depressed that it was over. *The Wire* is about life in the inner city of Baltimore, the world of crime and drugs, police, waterfront unions, schools, urban politics, and newspapers. It is down and dirty, dark and gloomy, yet humorous, and artistically successful as only large wallops of truth can be. It is as if Dickens was reborn and busied himself depicting life in Baltimore. But this series hits harder, and uses the advantages of television to do so. It woke us up to the possibility that television can be a transformational art form.

It is now apparent to me, some would say *finally* apparent to me, that while exceptional, *The Wire* is not an aberration and is part of something important. A few weeks ago, we finished watching all three seasons of *Deadwood*. Again, we did so over a small number of nights, looking forward to our daughter falling asleep so we could get on with the show. If you had told me that a television "western" could hold me that way, I would have never believed you. But as the *New York Times* wrote in March 2005, "*Deadwood* is a western the way *La Grande Illusion* was a war movie or *Vertigo* was a horror movie." The language is often Shakespearean, which would seem grossly out of place in that time and place but works beautifully. As does the swearing, which is both outrageous and constant. *Deadwood* portrays the West as a lawless territory where the meaner aspects of human character are far more on display than the occasional decency and honor. And, like *The Wire*, it packs the punch that television can provide.

Both shows are revisionist, both ask us to reconsider long-held views of the way things are in our cities and were in the West—that plays such a critical part in the American imagination. These shows offer a darker look at American life in the past and in the present, over many eras and in many different places and worlds. In Bate's context, these artists are standing on the shoulders of their predecessors to see and depict what was once glossed over, and to take advantage of the opportunities of their time—a heretofore underutilized medium.

This is the thesis of Brett Martin's new book, *Difficult Men–Behind the Scenes of a Creative Revolution: From The Sopranos and The Wire to Mad Men and Breaking Bad*. As Michiko Kakutani makes clear in her June 24 *New York Times* review, *Difficult Men* ambitiously posits that *The Sopranos* riffs off of the American fascination with the mob to get viewers to wrestle with their ambivalence about capitalism and their suspicion that "the American dream might at its core be a criminal enterprise." This could equally well be said for how *Deadwood* uses interest in the West and historical characters such as Wild Bill Hickok and Calamity Jane.

This past month we watched the first season of *Rectify*, which is about a forty-some-year-old man released from death row back to his family in a small Georgia town after DNA evidence raised doubts about his conviction for rape and murder nineteen years earlier. It is a slow-moving drama of character, which raises significant social, cultural, and political questions while also engaging your sympathy and your fears. As are *The Wire* and *Deadwood*, it is tough stuff. At the conclusion of the last episode, we sat, numb and scared, transformed by the power of art—and now of television—to help us see and feel the lives of other people, worlds apart from our own.

We are getting scant help from our political dialogue and most aspects of popular culture as we seek to understand what is happening in our country. Many aspects of mainstream media—video games, music, movies, and television—are indicative of a culture that seems to be slowly going mad. Alongside that dominant craziness might be the beginning of a "reckoning" of sorts, with our past and with the effects of steep economic decline, inequality, and class stratification. And how ironic, and also how American would it be, if that reckoning was delivered through the same vehicle—television—that likely contributed so much to the problem in the first place.

September 2013

MUSIC AND THE PLEASURES OF "LESSER LIGHTS"

THIS COLUMN SHOULD be entitled "Roosevelt Listens." Since readers are usually listeners as well, I trust you will bear with me.

I am struck by how some music becomes important at different times in life. For the last year a majority of the music on my CD player has been Baroque, although I had previously found that genre repetitive and unimaginative. I even failed to truly appreciate Bach. Now, much classical music from the Romantic era, Brahms and Chopin, and certainly Rachmaninoff, sounds excessively dramatic, over the top.

How can this music be so important to me when just a short time ago I could hardly abide it? Is it that with two highly stressful jobs in a row it provides a certain structure and peacefulness? Perhaps. Or perhaps I was just ready for it. That is true of many books. For full or sometimes any impact, you have to read them at the right time in your life.

In exploring Baroque and other classical music I am also struck by how much I enjoy works by composers who are relegated to the ranks of "lesser lights." Appreciation of classical music is declining, and orchestras increasingly play what they know will be familiar to their audience. That leaves a great deal of wonderful music unexplored.

My favorite composer for many years, Joseph Haydn, led me to my favorite among the lesser-knowns, Luigi Boccherini. I sought out Boccherini because of how often he is compared to Haydn, and

JOSEPH HAYDN: *KAISERLIED* (HOB XXVIA:43). CLEAN COPY OF A PIANO VERSION WITH THE FIRST STANZA. PERHAPS BETWEEN OCTOBER 1796 AND JANUARY 1797.
Joseph Haydn / Scan: Österreichische Nationalbibliothek

there are many similarities. Thankfully, these similarities include the fact that both composers led long, productive lives and left us large quantities of exceptional music.

Boccherini was born in Lucca, Italy, in 1743. (And what a lovely town that is. There is a statue of him there.) He went briefly to Vienna, but then moved on to Madrid. That move, far away from that era's musical epicenter, may account for his relative obscurity. He lived the rest of his life in various parts of Spain and died in poverty in 1805.

An accomplished cellist, he wrote a great deal of chamber music, including more than one hundred string quintets (one viola, two violins, and two cellos), an equal number of string quartets, thirty symphonies, and twelve magnificent cello concertos.

Some of his music reflects Spanish influences and so much of it is of such consistent melodic appeal, depth, and quality that one wonders why it is so little known.

Yet Boccherini is far better known than many of the Baroque composers I have grown to love. Most of them are also Italian. Are you familiar with Giuseppe Tartini? Neither was I. Tartini wrote spectacular violin concertos, at least 135 but perhaps as many as 200. In an age in which even very obscure music is available in just two days from Amazon, it is remarkable that a vast majority of these concertos are very hard to find. I am told that only 50 have ever been recorded.

What about Pietro Locatelli? His concerti grossi (concertos in which various instruments take the lead, later superseded by the solo instrument concerto) are magnificent. Arcangelo Corelli's equally wonderful concerti grossi are better known—after all it is a form he essentially invented. And then there are Giuseppe Torelli's spectacular violin concertos.

Many Baroque composers are famous—Vivaldi, Telemann, Purcell, Handel, and of course Bach. But the splendors of that era produced remarkable numbers of extraordinary composers who are hardly known today. Now that I have discovered them, I want to share my new passion with others.

If you are interested in exploring this music I can make a few recommendations on where to start. There are really wonderful recordings of Boccherini currently available at ridiculously low prices. I recommend Sony recordings of the cello concertos with Anner Bylsma on cello. At this time there is a five-CD box set which also includes several symphonies and string quintets available on Amazon for only $14.39. Buy it quickly.

But why stop there? Brilliant Classics has an expansive Boccherini box set of thirty-seven CDs for just $76.00. (Prices change often on these. I place them in my Amazon cart and watch as the prices fluctuate—acting quickly when they hit rock bottom.) A particularly fine full-price CD is *La musica notturna della strade di Madrid* by the Cuarteto Casals on Harmonia Mundi. This contains great recordings of some of Boccherini's more flamboyant music including his best known piece, the String Quintet in E Major.

As for Tartini, there are two excellent, reasonably easy-to-find recordings of some of his best violin concertos. On modern instruments, a Naxos CD with soloist Ariadne Daskalakis and the Cologne Chamber Orchestra is the best place to start. If you do not appreciate the first concerto on the disc, with its lovely slow movement, this music is likely not for you. On period instruments there is violinist Elizabeth Wallfisch's wonderful recording with the Raglan Baroque Players on Helios records. The Italian label L'arte Dell'arco has produced seventeen volumes of the concertos with violinist Giovanni Guglielmo, but these are hard to find and very expensive.

When I think of Tartini's many hard to find and unrecorded violin concertos, I reflect that Vivaldi's "The Four Seasons" has been recorded more than a thousand times. The artistic world increasingly mirrors the broader movement toward a "winner take all" society. In fact, the December issue of *Atlantic Magazine* reports that "the top 1% of bands and solo artists now earn 77% of all revenue from recorded music."

Were Boccherini and Tartini "lesser lights"? I am not sure who makes that judgment and what criteria they use. Perhaps they broke no new ground, but they created magnificently beautiful music that has stood the test of time and provides great solace to me as winter cold and greyness descend early and harshly on southwestern Ohio.

December 2014

BASEBALL

BASEBALL HAS BEEN a big part of my life since I attended Washington Senators games as young boy. I still affectionately remember the Senators' fine-fielding, poor-hitting shortstop Eddie Brinkman and their hulking outfielder Frank Howard. But when the Senators were lost to another city—not once, but twice—becoming the Minnesota Twins and then the Texas Rangers, I said enough of this and adopted the St. Louis Cardinals. At that point I became a *lucky* baseball fan.

Lucky because for most of the last five decades the Cardinals have been contenders, and there is not much I enjoy more than October baseball when they are "in the hunt." In 2011, they won a great seven-game World Series (over the Texas Rangers!) that included a game six comeback that ranks as one of the best and most unlikely ever played.

In 2014, for the fourth year in a row the Cardinals made it to the National League Championship Series, but for the second time in that stretch they lost to the San Francisco Giants. Another great run, and another chance to reflect on how tough it is to win it all, and how sad it is that only one team and its fans really get to celebrate. Why do folks enjoy finding fault with the "also rans," even if they were one of only four teams out of thirty still playing baseball in October?

Starting with Opening Day in April, baseball is like the weather. I check it every morning—peruse the Cardinals' box score and the standings and look to see who is pitching that day.

THE WASHINGTON SENATORS AT ROBERT F. KENNEDY
STADIUM IN WASHINGTON, D.C.
Marion S. Trikosko; Library of Congress

Then the season ends, adding to the melancholy that can accompany the end of summer. A. Bartlett Giamatti caught this beautifully in his essay "The Green Fields of the Mind." Baseball, he wrote, "breaks your heart. It is designed to break your heart. The game begins in the spring, when everything else begins again, and it blossoms in the summer, filling the afternoons and evenings, and then as soon as the chill rains come, it stops and leaves you to face the fall alone. You count on it, rely on it to buffer the passage of time, to keep the memory of sunshine and high skies alive, and then just when the days are all twilight, when you need it most, it stops."

Happily the wait is not that long. In mid-February, we will read that "pitchers and catchers report" (baseball fans consider those among the most beautiful four-word phrases in our language) to spring training, and the cycle begins again.

There are worrisome trends in the sport but also some positive ones. The big spending teams—the Yankees, Dodgers, Red Sox, and Angels—use their huge cable television contracts to significantly outspend smaller market teams—think Pittsburgh, Oakland, and Tampa Bay—but at least they pay a high-spenders' tax and more often than not are beaten out by their more frugal competitors. The National League still eschews the designated hitter: they still require pitchers to hit and managers to make hard choices on when to pinch hit for them. And artificial turf has almost disappeared, now used only at the ballparks of the Toronto Blue Jays and Tampa Bay Rays.

But the national audience is shrinking. The October 24, 2014 *New York Times* had a front page story entitled "It's Series Time, and Everybody's Watching…the Football Game." The first game of the Royals–Giants World Series was viewed by just 12.2 million. That same week more people watched the zombie cable show *The Walking Dead*, and twice as many people watched the United States versus Portugal in last summer's World Cup.

I think in part the loss of national viewership is due to the fact that the game is now so localized, as it is much easier to closely follow your favorite team regardless of where you live. I live in Cincinnati Reds country but since I subscribe to MLB TV, I can watch every Cardinals game. I read the *St. Louis Post-Dispatch* online and follow the Cardinals on several blogs, including the very good "Viva El Birdos" and "Fungoes: Cardinals News from a Sabermetric Point of View."

Heading into the off-season, one can always hold on to baseball through reading; baseball writing is plentiful and there is a great deal in fiction, essay, and biography that is very good. There are many lists of the best baseball literary works, so I will just mention a few that give me particular pleasure.

One is the long poem, "Casey at the Bat." The poem is good preparation for dealing with the sense of loss that is such a large part of being a baseball fan. It is also an unusual piece of American folklore, as it warns against hubris and overreaching.

Bang the Drum Slowly by Mark Harris is a lovely, bittersweet novel of a modestly talented catcher's last season. Dying of Hodgkin's disease, he wants one more go at it and unexpectedly contributes to his team's successful season. Not that quick mentally, he is often ridiculed. The narrator, his best friend on the team and a far better baseball player, ends the story saying, "From here on in I rag nobody." Perhaps not a great novel, it is a highly affecting one that was made into an equally gentle and generous movie, with Robert De Niro playing against type in the lead role.

Other favorites include the poet Donald Hall's essays, *Fathers Playing Catch with Sons*, and his biography of Dock Ellis, *In the Country of Baseball*; Jane Leavy's biographies of Sandy Koufax and

Mickey Mantle; Larry Tye's biography of Satchel Paige; Jules Tygiel on Jackie Robinson; and David Halberstam's *October 1964*, which recounts the Cardinals' 1964 World Series victory over the New York Yankees.

And then there is John Updike's essay on Ted Williams' last game, "Hub Fans Bid Kid Adieu." In his final at-bat Williams hit a home run, getting the kind of rhyming ending that eludes almost all of us. But it's not the home run that makes the story, but rather Williams' distance from the fans, a distance he will not compromise.

"Like a feather caught in a vortex, Williams ran around the bases at the center of our beseeching screaming. He ran as he always ran out home runs—hurriedly, unsmiling, head down, as if our praise were a storm of rain to get out of. He didn't tip his cap. Though we thumped, wept, and chanted, 'We want Ted' for minutes after he hid in the dugout, he did not come back. Our noise for some seconds passed beyond excitement into a kind of immense open anguish, a wailing, a cry to be saved. But immortality is nontransferable. The papers said that the other players, and even the umpires on the field, begged him to come out and acknowledge us in some way, but he refused. Gods do not answer letters."

Now that I have written about baseball maybe I can let the season pass and move on. Maybe I will stop talking about the Cardinals to workmates and others who endure my passion for the game and that team with good humor. But know that I do not think that baseball is a small thing, but rather a great gift I inherited as an American.

Near the end of his life, Updike wrote a short afterword for the 50th anniversary edition of his Williams essay. He noted that Williams had returned to Fenway Park near his own death and "made a show of tipping his cap to the crowd; but we didn't need that. The crowd and Ted always shared what was important, a belief that this boy's game terrifically mattered."

It does.

As the Kansas City Royals celebrated their return to the World Series after twenty-nine years, one of the pleasures was watching Royals star George Brett in the stands celebrating with as much joy as a young fan. Asked in a television interview if he could explain what the Royals resurgence means to Kansas City, Brett said it might be helpful if he talked about his own family. He spoke about his three sons, all in their twenties, all blessed by good fortune and opportunity. He said that after the Royals clinched a spot in the playoffs, one of his sons told him that he had never been happier, never had more fun.

I wish they had won it all.

November 2014

HOLIDAY THOUGHTS—"WHAT WE NEED IS HERE"

THE HOLIDAY SEASON was designed to provide rest and relaxation and some time for worship and spiritual reflection. At least I think it was, but that is a distant memory. December has become a frenetic month. The commercialization of the holidays is so pervasive that it is difficult to hold on to what might still be healthy. All that keeps my family from tuning it out entirely is that our eight-year-old daughter, Juliana, is so excited. And while that excitement has much to do with the prospect of gifts, it is also tied to certain sweet rituals such as decorating the tree and preparing for Santa's descent down the chimney.

At the office and at home, and now on email, holiday cards pour in from work associates, vendors, would-be vendors, and politicians. The sentiments may be laudable, but when sent to hundreds or even thousands with address labels, printed signatures, and bulk rate postage, they retain little power to affect the spirit.

And seasonal demands to purchase are everywhere. It amuses me that many equate today's turbo-charged capitalism with "conservatism." In fact, modern commercial capitalism is perhaps the least conservative force in the history of the world. Capitalism is carnivorously unsentimental and non-ideological. If you doubt this, just watch as various established companies and entrepreneurs swoop in as commerce opens up with Cuba. Commercialism has been gorging on the "spirit of Christmas" for decades now.

Yet even if it is difficult to find the time and space for reflection, it does not mean that it is not available.

Reading provides one avenue.

And reading may be even more salutary than we thought. The December 21 Sunday *New York Times* contains an article entitled "How Reading Transforms Us" by Keith Oatley and Maja Djikic. I have often struggled to defend my belief that it matters not only that we read but *what* we read. That view is arguably snobbish. But Oatley and Djikic offer new research that it is defensible—that it is *quality* stories, both factual and fictional, that catalyze changes in personality. They write, "Those who read a story or essay that they judged to be artistic changed their personality scores significantly more than those who judged what they read to be less artistic." This is a new area of study—"outside the domain of love relationships and some forms of psychotherapy, the idea of communication that has effects of a non-persuasive yet transformative kind has rarely been considered in psychology." We have long known that advertising products can influence behavior; it is now possible to hope that literature can provide at least a partial counterbalancing.

A Christmas Carol and even *The Grinch Who Stole Christmas* may be terribly out of date in seeing "scrooges" as the most powerful threat to an authentic Christmas spirit, but if you are looking for signs of how an indomitable spirit can overcome hardship—that, too, is readily available. The December 21 *New York Times* also has an article in the *Sunday Magazine* about "The Unbreakable Laura Hillenbrand."

And what a story it is. Her ability to craft spectacular tales of unlikely triumph, despite her own debilitating illness, an illness—chronic fatigue syndrome—that was often not even acknowledged, is as inspiring as *It's a Wonderful Life* might have been the first time you saw it as a child.

There are many other seasonal offerings to embrace. Some of the best Christmas stories implore us to hold commercialism at bay. That is the message of *A Charlie Brown Christmas*, which also provides some of the most addictive jazzy Christmas music. And in 1978 Raymond Briggs published *The Snowman*, a book without words that was made into a film with no dialogue in 1982. Briggs introduces it this way: "I remember that winter because it had brought the heaviest snows I had ever seen. Snow had fallen steadily all night long and in the morning I woke in a room filled with light and silence, the whole world seemed to be held in a dream-like stillness. It was a magical day…and it was on that day I made the Snowman."

The Snowman is good to slow things down.

So is poetry. Galway Kinnell died this past year. He had a long, productive life and wrote well about physical pleasures and love of the natural world, including this late poem:

Astonishment

Oarlocks knock in the dusk, a rowboat rises
and settles, surges and slides.
Under a great eucalyptus,
a boy and girl feel around with their feet
for those small flattish stones so perfect
for scudding across the water.

A dog barks from the deep in the silence.
A woodpecker, double-knocking,
keeps time. I have slept in so many arms.
Consolation? Probably. But too much
consolation may leave one inconsolable.

The water before us has hardly moved
except in the shallowest breathing places.
For us back then, to live seemed almost to die.
One day a darkness fell between her and me.
When we woke, a hawthorn sprig
stood in the water glass at our bedside.

There is a silence in the beginning.
The life within us grows quiet.
There is a little fear. No matter
how all this comes out, from now on

it cannot exist ever again.
We liked talking our nights away
in words close to the natural language,
which most other animals can still speak.

The present pushes back the life of regret.
It draws forward the life of desire. Soon memory
will have started sticking itself all over us.
We were fashioned from clay in a hurry,
poor throwing may mean it didn't matter
to the makers if their pots cracked.

On the mountain tonight the full moon
faces the full sun. Now could be the moment
when we fall apart or we become whole.
Our time seems to be up—I think I even hear it stopping.
Then why have we kept up the singing for so long?
Because that's the sort of determined creatures we are.
Before us, our first task is to astonish,
and then, harder by far, to be astonished.

Wendell Berry also writes beautifully about our relationship to nature. Berry turned eighty this year, and, as he was good enough to visit Antioch to support the College as we explore more sustainable ways of living, let's give him the last word:

The Wild Geese

Horseback on Sunday morning,
harvest over, we taste persimmon
and wild grape, sharp sweet
of summer's end. In time's maze
over fall fields, we name names
that went west from here, names
that rest on graves. We open
a persimmon seed to find the tree
that stands in promise,
pale, in the seed's marrow.
Geese appear high over us,
pass, and the sky closes. Abandon,
as in love or sleep, holds
them to their way, clear,
in the ancient faith: what we need
is here. And we pray, not
for new earth or heaven, but to be
quiet in heart, and in eye
clear. What we need is here.

January 2015

MARK ROOSEVELT
PRESIDENT, ANTIOCH COLLEGE

Mark Roosevelt has been involved with various aspects of education reform for nearly 30 years. As chairman of the Massachusetts state legislature's Education Committee, he authored the Education Reform Act of 1993, which fundamentally changed how that state funds and organizes its public schools. He also served as superintendent of the Pittsburgh Public Schools, where, among other initiatives, he created The Pittsburgh Promise, which guarantees up to $10,000 a year in college funding for high school graduates and has sent more than 5,000 students to college.

As president of Antioch College, Roosevelt has recruited a stellar faculty of scholar-practitioners who are dedicated to teaching; admitted high-capacity, idealistic students—a large number of whom come from challenging economic circumstances; began the renovation of the college's historic 160-year-old campus; and revitalized the most robust cooperative education program in the country.

"Over the years, whenever I saw Mark, I would ask what he was reading. I would get a far-ranging list of fiction and nonfiction for which he provided a lively, intelligent, and witty commentary. I am delighted that, in this wonderful book, he is sharing his remarkable insights, which are bound to trigger conversations and controversies. These are brilliant essays by a voracious life-long reader. This volume invites us to engage in a new way with our own reading experiences."

—ALAN BRINKLEY
Renowned historian, author and professor of history at Columbia University